WOMAN

Books by Joyce Brothers

WOMAN

10 DAYS TO A SUCCESSFUL MEMORY
(with Edward Eagan)

WOMAN

BY DR. JOYCE BROTHERS

DOUBLEDAY & COMPANY, INC., GARDEN CITY, NEW YORK

1961

Contents

WOMAN

Part One

THE SINGLE WOMAN

CHAPTER ONE

What Is Love?

IN ONE sense, at least, all human beings are unquestionably created equal. For each and every one of us needs love. That such a universal requirement should be so hard to define, so often misunderstood, and, for many, so hard to find is a curious paradox. But whatever the problems of definition, of recognition, of search, the truth is inescapable that men and women must have love, must give love and receive love if they are to fulfill themselves as complete human beings and infuse their lives with meaning.

One of the difficulties in trying to pin down and analyze love is that, since it is so commonly used as a noun, one tends to suppose it is a tangible object, a *thing*. But in reality, in terms of our practical experience, it is more properly a process, a matter of active feeling and behavior. It is not so much a question of what love *is* as of what love *does*. And while this book is primarily addressed to women, it would be misleading to suggest that love as a functional human necessity operates one way for men and another way for women.

13

It is true that a man is likely to express his need for love — his feelings of love — in ways that differ from a woman's. But the sooner that we, as women, recognize that men have the same needs we have for the reassurance, the trust, the security of affection that are the core of love, the sooner we will end the battle between the sexes and arrive at greater mutual satisfaction and happiness.

A man, by virtue of his physical strength and his freedom from childbearing with all its ramifications, is conditioned to take the initiative and to refrain from showing fear, hesitation, dependence, or weakness. He is supposed to go out and seek love, just as he is supposed to go out and provide food, and yet he is not expected to be so soft as to confess his need. As a result, men have a tendency to grab at what looks promising — and then, in silence, hope it will turn out to be love. Women, on the other hand, are supposed to have fodder brought to them, to be protected and sought after. They are *not* to take the initiative, even though they run the risk of being branded as spinsters. So they wait and hope for love and try not to appear anxious, and then, too often in desperation, they grab at what is available. The difference between men and women is basically one of timing, of initiative, of articulateness and social manners. Underneath, women crave — and flourish on — the same essential emotional diet.

Still, it appears to be women who need a greater measure of comfort and guidance in the realm of love. Perhaps it is partly because of that restriction against taking the initiative. And perhaps it is partly because it is not considered unwomanly — as it might be considered unmanly for men —

to give serious thought and attention to this crucial aspect of life. In any event, there's no denying that the well-being and happiness of most women depend on achieving a satisfying and lasting relationship with a man, which means achieving the ultimate fulfillment of love. In writing this book I hope that by trying to help some women toward a clearer understanding of the nature of love, of their own needs, of ways in which love may be given and received — and held — I'll also be helping them to a fuller knowledge of men, and so to that shared ultimate fulfillment.

Fortunately, all of us are born with the capacity to love. In the words of a well-known song, it comes naturally. Unfortunately, many things can happen to us from infancy on that may reduce or even destroy that natural capacity and also render us unable to receive love. But it's the unique and miraculous nature of love to be infinite and ever self-regenerating. The simple but observable fact is that the more you love, the more you are able to love. We cannot even count love's forms or manifestations. That's one of the troubles when we attempt to define it. There is the love of a parent for a child, of a child for a parent, of brothers and sisters; there is the selfless, sexless love of a friend, of a teacher, of a minister, priest, or rabbi; there is the love of nature and freedom; and there is the love of God. The term is also applied to music, to painting, to a favorite book. And it has been degraded with use for everything from popcorn to mink. Despite misuse and confusion and multiplicity, however, it is still possible — and vital — to consider love as the dynamic force that draws and binds adult males and females together.

15

Woman

In this sense, love occurs only when a person is ready for it, prepared physically and emotionally for its inception. At this point it may develop slowly, growing over a long acquaintance, and so be relatively easy to recognize. But sometimes it comes quickly, and then there's the problem of differentiating between love and infatuation. I have found that it isn't only young girls who have trouble telling the two apart. Women of all ages run into this difficulty, and since love is a process rather than an entity, it is probably best defined in terms of contrasts, of what it doesn't do as well as what it does do. So let's start with this common dilemma regarding love and infatuation. How *do* you tell the difference?

Some of the best minds in social counseling have tried to produce tests that the ordinary woman can apply to help her decide whether an attraction to another person is genuine or merely a short-term imitation. Of course such tests are useless unless the "victim" of a powerful emotion really wants the answer. Unfortunately, the very nature of infatuation usually keeps a woman from wanting to test it. Love, painful though it may be at times, is a precious emotion. And even an ersatz version is hard to give up. Trying to convince a woman that what she feels is not the real and lasting variety is usually a waste of time — after all, how can somebody else know what's going on inside her? — while to suggest that she may be motivated by disappointment or self-pity may only provoke resentment and defiance.

However, if you think you are in love, if you are contemplating marriage and would seriously like to determine your chances of happiness in such a marriage, the tests are available. You can ask yourself certain questions. If you answer them honestly, you'll get an inkling of the nature of your emotional entanglement; and, if you are wise and strong-minded, you may even be able to save yourself from a serious mistake.

The first question is: Do you and this man want the same things out of life?

For example, high on the list of mutual aims that a man and woman who love each other want to share are, of course, children. If one person thinks of marriage as a perpetual honeymoon without the intrusion of children, while the other visualizes a half dozen young replicas of the loved one running around the house, the result is sure to be unhappiness.

Another mutual aim is a settled home. If one partner in a marriage expects to lead the life of a gypsy king, wandering from one carefree adventure to another, and the other dreams of a snug vine-covered cottage, the prospects for a lasting union are again unlikely.

The third mutual aim concerns money. If one partner has a powerful urge for monetary success, while the other considers it unimportant, there may be trouble ahead. If one partner wants shiny cars and fancy clothes, while the other prefers to put money in the bank, there may well be bitter quarrels.

The second question to ask yourself is related to the first but is much more specific.

We expect a strong physical attraction to exist between people in love. They look forward to years of satisfactory marital relations. But do you have any *other* interests in common, or is physical love all you share?

Physical love is important. But that is not all. If you do not have similar tastes, if you do not like to talk about the same kinds of things, if you do not enjoy the same kinds of outings or the same friends, you are headed for bickering unless you have an above-average ability to be tolerant and yielding to your partner's set of values. And a relationship based purely on physical attraction can become painfully dull and even tragic as the years go by.

Make a list of your interests in recreation, social activity, and so on. See if these match the interests of your prospective husband. If more than half of them do not match, the emotion you feel is probably infatuation and not real love.

Then, as a final test, try for a moment to analyze your real attitude toward the physical side. What if the one you think you love were seriously injured, perhaps even disfigured? Would you still feel the same toward him?

The third big question to ask yourself concerns your sense of humor. I know every woman believes she has a sense of humor. However, do you and the one you believe you love, laugh at the same things?

A young and inexperienced person may not realize how important it is to be able to "laugh things off." This is vital in a marriage. If a couple share a sense of humor, they can usually manage to overcome any difference they may have over the problems that are bound to arise in normal life. But if one person finds things boring and disagreeable that the other regards as hilariously funny, the pair will have a hard time finding a common ground.

The fourth question is: Do you expect to reform this person? You may believe that you love him in spite of his faults, but do you have in the back of your mind the notion that after you are married you will help him overcome his weaknesses?

This is a poor basis for marriage in several respects. In the first place, if you do not wholeheartedly respect a person, if you secretly suspect he is weak, what you feel for him can hardly be true love. And the fact that you have chosen such a person indicates an emotional weakness in yourself that does not augur well for your stability when things get dark in the future.

In the second place, if the faults you recognize in your prospective partner are real, it is most unlikely, as experience fortified by recent experimental studies have demonstrated, that you will change him by marriage. A habit of heavy drinking, for example, is rarely cured by love alone, no matter how great that love may be. So don't count on making over your mate after the wedding.

Your own emotional stability has a great deal to do with resolving the question of love versus infatuation. Of course it is always difficult to decide for yourself how emotionally stable you are. But scientists have discovered that family background gives us a good indication of the level of stability of individuals.

One of the best tests, in fact, for the possibilities of a happy marriage is whether both the man and woman have parents who are happily married. When young people think they are in love, they are far less likely to be fooling themselves if they have a sound idea of what true love really is, and they will have that idea if they have seen true love in their own homes. Therefore, an important question is: Are his parents, as well as your own, happily married?

Finally, scientific observers have developed one generally conclusive item in the test to distinguish love from infatuation. To apply it, ask yourself this:

Can you — that is, both of you — discuss frankly and without fear or resentment the details of your mutual feelings? Can you sit down with a third party — a doctor, a minister, a marriage counselor, or even a respected friend — and bring into the open, clearly and without entangling emotions, your fears and hopes and doubts about one another? If you can do this, it is a good sign of the genuineness of your love and of your emotional maturity as well as your prospective husband's.

A childish person or an infatuated one — and they are generally the same thing — cannot talk about her feelings in this way. She gets all worked up. She feels hurt and resentful when doubts about her are expressed. She feels embarrassed at discussing physical relations with the man she intends to marry. The same is true of men. If your prospective husband squirms and cannot carry this test through, then look for trouble ahead. You must be honest with yourself if you think you are in love.

I know of a woman in her thirties who had never been in love or even infatuated. Since her college days she had worked in one department store. She was calm, capable, and extremely efficient. Although she was attractive, she had never let down the bars that can lead to love.

After nearly fifteen years with the department store, she

20

was made an executive. She had achieved what is generally regarded as a high degree of success, but suddenly she realized that material success had not brought her the happiness she desired.

Dissatisfied, she met a young man — much younger than she — and began seeing a great deal of him. She found herself floundering in a sea of her own emotions. She thought she was in love, but she was not sure.

Nevertheless, she married the young man in question — a man she sensed to be completely worthless and whom she knew was much younger and vain. The result was foreseeable. She was desperately unhappy. Such a marriage could not and did not last. For marriage, like any other successful partnership, must be built on a solid foundation, not just on sex and the romance of being married.

That brings us to another vital phase in understanding the nature of love — the difference between love and sex. Is there any difference, and how can we be sure that what we think is love is not merely a simple biological urge?

Sex and love are like tea and milk. They can be mixed or they can be taken straight. Each has certain distinctive characteristics, but when they are combined they form a unique substance. It is easy to confuse love and sex when you are in a state of intense infatuation; and the answer is to cool off a bit. If there is any doubt at all in your mind, refrain from seeing the one you think you love for a short time.

Sex is as much a part of a normal marriage relationship as is love. Sex is complementary to love and is most gratifying when performed in an atmosphere of love. But that

21

does not make them the same. I know a number of women who have admitted that they have been attracted to men — have even had sexual relations with them — in the full knowledge that they did not love them. They were excited by these men, but it was purely a physical excitement. They had little pleasure from their relationship, I am sure. They may have received physical satisfaction — the relief that flows from the consummation of the sex act. But for woman, to a greater degree than for a man, it often seems, sex is truly rewarding only when it is an expression of love; it is but a part of the enjoyment of living together. Indulgence in the sex act for the physical pleasure alone can lead a woman to self-doubt, to frustration, and even to serious mental disturbance. For sex alone does not gratify a woman's need for love.

That is not to denigrate sex as an integral part of living. In the course of two or three generations we have shifted to a position directly opposite that held by earlier generations. Earlier, even in marriage, sexual pleasure for a woman was considered a sin. The sex act was a necessary duty that a woman performed in exchange for the security of her home and her children.

Today we understand sexual experience as an expression of both love and physical desire. Let me make it clear, however, that, for a woman, sex is just one incident in a whole sequence of events: pregnancy, childbirth, breast feeding, and child care. For a man, sex can exist for its own sake, and the sex act is ended with orgasm. Therefore, a woman cannot be expected, despite all the new emphasis on her participation in the sex act, to have a psychological attitude toward sex that is identical to that of a man. Sex is not love, and it can never take the place of love in the emotional needs of any woman.

Love is a much more complicated matter than sex. Indeed, it is perhaps the most complicated of all human emotions. The underside of love, the side we do not care to look at, sometimes seeps through to show us just how complicated an emotion we have to deal with, and one of the ways we can examine love is by looking at the wrong side. There we find jealousy. This emotion, ignoble as we may believe it, is a part of love.

Are you jealous? That doesn't necessarily mean you are in love. But if you *are* in love, you are jealous. Perhaps you do not admit it even to yourself. Perhaps you control it so admirably that no one ever suspects. Yet jealousy exists as a simple affirmation of love. You are not jealous when you do not care; you are jealous only when you are emotionally involved. You can be envious of someone you do not love, but that is quite a different thing. To be jealous, you must have a feeling of involvement and possession.

Jealousy is a perfectly normal emotion. I am frequently jealous of some of my husband's pretty patients. I can tell (and how I can tell I really don't know) the moment he has a pretty woman patient on the telephone. I may be at the other end of the house, but when he gets a certain tone in his voice I know he is talking to a pretty woman. And whatever I am doing, I pause while the twinge of jealousy comes over me.

Jealousy is an emotion you can't always avoid, but you can help yourself and others by knowing more about its causes and how to cope with it. Some people think that jealousy is cute or adorable. It is not. It is potentially dangerous. I have known of parents, oblivious of its destructive force, who encourage it in their children. For example, a father will say something like, "Watch how jealous Johnny gets when I make a fuss over the baby," and despite any protest he will proceed to demonstrate.

It is understandable that in the close relationships of marriage and family life there is always much jealousy. But in the long run, uncontrolled jealousy spells unhappiness and sometimes deep tragedy for all who are touched by it. So let us try to understand it better and discuss ways in which it may be checked.

Jealousy is not simple. Resentment, suspicion, and envy all come into it in varying degrees. The situations in which jealousy usually appears are those in which other persons or things seem to possess the love, prestige, approval, or attention that one wants for oneself. When some people don't get the positive recognition they desire they may be driven to the purely negative response of jealousy. The jealousy may be an overpowering emotional experience — even one that blocks out other feelings and thoughts — or it may be a constant, gnawing kind of anxiety.

Whatever its form, jealousy is the expression of an insecure and childish person, and when I am having a pang of jealousy I am treating myself to a bit of the child in me.

Actually, jealousy is childish in a double sense. In the first place, the roots of jealousy extend back into childhood relationships with parents and brothers and sisters, although the jealous one may be entirely unaware of or have for-

24

gotten the source. Second, it causes childish behavior as a device — a very primitive device — for gaining the desired affection, approval, or attention.

Since none of us wants to appear foolish and immature or to court danger, it behooves us to make a determined effort to overcome this debilitating emotion. Here are some tips:

First, spend more time in actively seeking adult methods of gaining love or approval or attention than in merely trying to control your jealousy. Childish satisfactions are much more likely to be dropped when you find more adequate adult satisfactions.

Second, remember that you, as a jealous person, must practice emotional independence. As you gradually gain self-confidence you will not be so completely lost at the times when you do not have the attention of the one you love. Develop your skills, your activities, your sense of achievement. One suggestion I have found helpful is to become an expert in one area, no matter how small.

As you become more confident and acquire more faith in your own ability, praise will be less important to you. The more secure you become, the more likely you are to get the affection and attention you want. In an emotional sphere, the rich do get richer and the poor get poorer.

When you perceive jealousy in another, unless you are directly responsible for the behavior of the jealous one, it is best not to attempt any direct interference or advice. Parents have a right to intercede because they must assume responsibility for their children's psychological welfare. Counselors and therapists are sometimes in a position to be a substitute parent and therefore help. But others, including *wives*, had better *not* try a direct approach to jealousy.

You may even need self-protection from the jealous one. And here the rule is: Don't let the jealous one control your behavior by his jealousy. If your prospective husband is jealous, keep your own counsel. Make no attempt to "cure" him, but, on the other hand, don't let him bully you. Since you know that he is seeking love or approval, give him all the recognition and affection you can at times when he is not showing jealousy. But don't overdo your attention. Be consistent in the attention you give a jealous person. Overly proud, overly possessive, and overly competitive people are insecure, and insecurity is often expressed by jealousy. The tragedy is that nothing *but* tragedy lies ahead in life for those who never learn how to handle their own painful and destructive jealousy.

One young woman sought my help not long ago because she *knew* she must rise above her jealousy, yet she was extremely jealous of her fiancé — after two and a half years. She thought he loved her, but she could not refrain from picking arguments about other girls he had gone out with in the past. When he saw one of these girls on the street, he would wave or stop and talk to her. Some of them, the unhappy girl said, acted as though he were still dating them.

My suggestion to this girl was that she first reassure herself of her fiancé's true motives. Was he intentionally trying to make her jealous, or was he acting in a normal, friendly way? In other words, she must first determine whether or not his intentions were proper. If he was trying to make her jealous, that was a warning sign. This type of sadistic behavior never adds to marital happiness, and it may be a first symptom of a series of actions designed to persecute the girl and satisfy the man's actual hatred for women.

But if he was just behaving in a normal, friendly way, she could find this out by asking him to be a little less cordial, explaining that it would make her more comfortable. If his intentions were harmless, he would not mind doing this at all.

This was truly a period of crisis for the young girl in question. If she waited until after she was married, her jealousy could ruin their happiness. With the responsibilities of a home and children, it would become even more important for her to be assured of her husband's love. If she were to doubt her ability, her attractiveness and then all of her marital relationships would be affected, including her sexual experience. Her brooding on her jealousy could create a mental image of her husband that was entirely unfair to him, could turn her against him completely. Obviously their marriage would have little chance of survival.

When you are dealing with jealousy, your own or that of the man you want to marry, you must weigh the matter very carefully. In your own case, you must be able to say: "I am just the kind of girl this boy wants and needs. No one could be a more loving or better wife to him. He knows we will have a wonderful life together, so there's no reason for him even to consider another girl."

If the jealousy is on the other side and you cannot bring it under control, you had better look elsewhere for a mate. The relationship between man and wife is so intimate, so closely woven of many factors, that it cannot survive in an atmosphere of suspicion and tension.

Though jealousy is another side of love — an ugly side — it is by no means the only other side. In fact, one of the most remarkable features about a mature person's capacity for love is that it is limitless. A parent's love for one child does not bar or cut down his love for the other children. It is a wondrous gift. But it has its troublesome ramifications too. Contrary to popular belief, it is quite possible, emotionally as well as biologically, for a woman to love two men at the same time or for a man to love more than one woman. Therein lies the source of many a dilemma, many a tragedy. Perhaps we would be better able to avoid the dangers and heartbreaks, however, if we regarded this facet of love as a challenge, an opportunity, an affirmation of love's positive qualities.

Certainly one of the nobler elements of love — and it is actually a criterion of genuine love — is its selflessness. By this I mean that love implies your willingness to *give* without thought of return or other consequence. The giving will be of the best in yourself — your loyalty, your honesty, your unwavering devotion. And sometimes it will mean a sacrifice on your part — your plans for an evening put aside in favor of his, or a new hat forsworn in order to buy him something you know he wants or needs. These are relatively minor sacrifices, to be sure. The most extreme sacrifice, of course, is to give one's life for the sake of another. In a middle and more commonly experienced area is the sacrifice of alternative satisfaction — in short, the decision to limit the expression of your love to the one with whom you have exchanged vows of constancy.

Monogamy is the way of life in our Judeo-Christian society, and in many ways it is women who uphold it most strongly, for it is more important, necessary, and possibly more natural to women than to men. Recent surveys make clear that the monogamous relationship is sometimes maintained only on the surface. Nevertheless, by a process of trial and error Western civilization has given legal, moral, and religious sanction to monogamy, which has been defined as the legal and religious union of a man and woman. It is considered an ethical ideal which provides the most stable relationship among mature people. And one of the tests of maturity is the ability to live comfortably within society's rules. So it is an attribute of both love and maturity — part of the implicit bond between them — for a woman to cleave only unto her husband. In any event, when a woman follows the *rules* of civilization she has a greater possibility of achieving contentment and happiness.

Most of us manage to curb — to control — our feelings of desire for more than one person of the opposite sex if we have them. We work them out in socially accepted ways, because leading a double life is difficult, for one thing. It creates enormous feelings of guilt, which are extremely painful to live with. For the single woman who may love two men at once, the problem is rather different: Which one shall she marry? Here time has a way of helping us arrive at a judgment, and in the chapters that follow I have attempted to add some useful suggestions.

Meanwhile, the main thing for any woman to remember is that love is the essence of her happiness. Life without love would be at best a kind of half life. We cannot be happy while we are lonely. To be sure, not one of us ever knows all the thoughts and emotions that surge through the breast of another. But none of us can exist fulfilled unless we love. Love is our escape route from isolation and unhappiness, and if it is an illusion, as some have said, it is an illusion without which men as well as women could not bear to live. Don't shy away from it, mistreat it, or underestimate it.

CHAPTER TWO

How Can I Be Popular?

WHEN I was a high school girl in Laurelton, Long Island, I decided that the thing that meant more to me than anything else in the world was to be popular. So I went to the public library and read everything I could get my hands on about popularity and personality. Norman Vincent Peale was not generally known then, as he is now, and the emphasis was not so much on confident living as on the Dale Carnegie approach. But I remember the single book that most impressed me — a teen-ager — was called *Susan, Be Smooth*. That's all I can remember about the book. I read it. I remembered it. And I set out to be smooth, which in those days was the most a girl could be.

Although I was far from the prettiest girl in the class, I found that when I discovered one great secret of teen-age popularity I became a success. That secret is *confidence*.

A teen-ager is in between. She is neither child nor woman. She wants to be both, at different times even during the same day. But more, she wants to be a woman and is constantly experimenting with the trappings of womanhood.

31

She experiments with make-up, with her hair, and with her clothes. She practices different ways of walking, talking, and even eating.

All teen-agers are conformists, although in the eyes of adult society they may appear to be rebels, for they huddle together against the common enemies of the adult world. But the teen-agers who are leaders, who are popular with their schoolmates, are those who do something just a little bit different. I say "a little bit" advisedly. No teen-ager becomes popular by stepping so far out of the mold as to be weird. It is all right to be a straight-A student, but not a bookworm. It is all right to be a bit daring, but not too daring. The idea is to do something to stand out but still stay within the pattern of the teen-age world.

My solution at one time was to wear slacks to a party. Does that sound silly? From an adult point of view it was silly, but from a teen-age point of view it was an extremely effective way of calling attention to myself as a leader among my schoolmates. In those days girls always wore skirts and sweaters to parties. After I appeared in slacks, at the next party all the girls wore slacks. And then, once the fad got going, I made sure I was the first to drop it and return to wearing skirts and sweaters to parties.

It was a fad, just as loafer shoes or black-and-white saddle shoes or wooden shoes become fads. And of course as a fad it was simply a form of rebellion against the adult world. Teen-agers want to rebel together, and it is important that no one step too far forward without encouragement from the group.

That, in a nutshell, is the secret of teen popularity. But

if you think about it for a moment you will realize that it is not so far removed from the adult world. Of course there is no room for the same degree of exaggeration in the adult world, but do you recall the sack dress of a few years ago and the balloon skirt of the following season? These were fads in the adult world, and the women who followed them were using the fad to seek attention and popularity.

For teens and for adult women, the secret of popularity is the same: confidence. When a woman is confident, she exudes an aura. All of us have seen an attractive woman walking down the street who seems to have a certain *something*. She may not be the prettiest woman. She may not be chic. She may even be dressed inexpensively. But there is something in her bearing, something in the way she walks, that shouts her confidence. She is a pleasure to watch, and men, in particular, will find her a pleasure to know.

It is one thing to say "Be confident!" It is quite another thing to take the steps that will lead to real confidence.

Many people have the feeling that they just can't do things right. This is a feeling that very often starts in childhood when perfection is demanded of the child — either by the parent or the teacher — and the child feels that unless something is done perfectly it should never be done at all. Because perfection can never be reached, the child who has such an impossible goal set for her grows up with a feeling of failure — of not being a worthwhile person. This pervades the individual's whole life, crippling her even to the point where she is unable to make decisions about the everyday activities of life.

One woman I know who had been brought up by a perfectionist mother was torn by indecision. Because she did not consider herself a worthy person, she could not believe that her decisions were worthwhile or correct. Whatever she bought for her home or for her children or for herself seemed wrong, and she felt she should have done better. Her new carpeting didn't seem to tie in with her furniture, although it seemed just right in the store. She had her dining-room chairs reupholstered several times. She even found her vacations ruined by the thought that she could have had a better time elsewhere. Finally she found herself at the point where she was afraid to buy anything, go anywhere, or see anyone.

This is an extreme case, but it illustrates the point for every woman.

When you lack confidence, you are not alone. Everyone has some feeling of inferiority. It may be continuous or occasional, but even the most confident people have occasional twinges of oversensitiveness, frustration, timidity, inadequacy, uncertainty, and doubts about their ability. None of us can escape this sense of fear or danger. In a limited sense it serves a definite function. Progress often stems from dissatisfaction with oneself and surroundings.

We are almost like Achilles, who was held by the heel and dipped into the river Styx. As a gift from the gods, he was protected from physical harm. The only place he was vulnerable was where the water had not touched his heel.

We are all granted safety from psychological danger in varying degrees. Everyone has an Achilles' heel, but some of us are vulnerable in many other places too. Many people create their own vulnerabilities by underestimating their capacities and capabilities. They sell themselves short.

I remember the story of a pilot who was forced down in the wilds of Alaska. Weeks later he walked into a frontier town. After he had eaten and rested he was shown a map of the area and saw how far he had walked. His reaction was: "It's impossible. I just couldn't have done it."

This man did not believe in his capacity and capability even after it had been demonstrated. Had he known about all of the rivers, the mountain ranges, the swamps he had to fight his way through when he *started* his walk, he might have said: "I can never make it." It is quite possible that he never would have.

The truth is, we never know our capacity until it is challenged. We can, of course, make some estimate by analyzing and comparing. If you undervalue yourself, how can you reasonably expect others to increase the valuation?

I am sure there are times when you get into a social situation that makes you wish you could simply vanish. The palms of your hands are damp, your pulse beats faster, you have difficulty breathing, and your body trembles. This is such a painful experience that most people will do almost anything to avoid it.

What can *you* do to get over this feeling? First, compare yourself with others. You will generally find you are as pretty, as graceful, and as intelligent as your companions. Observe closely and you will see that even the most admirable have faults. Your second step might be to make people like you because you are interested in them. And

35

the more you listen, the better they will like and admire you.

After a while you will have a better knowledge of the world, and then you can better estimate your capacities and decide where they need strengthening. Each day you will be dipping yourself a little deeper into the protective stream of experience. Finally you will cover the most sensitive areas with a thicker skin of self-confidence. You will always have some tender spots, but the protection will be nearly complete.

To gain confidence, we must realize that everyone makes mistakes. The only people who don't make mistakes are those who don't do anything. If you sit around the house all day doing absolutely nothing, calling no one, seeing no one, then possibly nothing will go wrong. You will never feel slighted, because no one will hurt you. They won't even know you exist.

A man I know who holds an executive position in a large firm has often said he is much happier knowing that his employees make some mistakes, since he always felt that if an employee never made a mistake he was probably shirking his job.

So in the search for confidence, don't forget, you have to keep moving. You have no time to feel sorry for yourself. Every one of us has troubles, and every one of us makes mistakes with people.

To be popular, of course, you have to make friends. It was Dale Carnegie who pointed out that the greatest winner of friends is a puppy. The reason for this is that a dog will go out of his way to show how much he likes you. And that is the secret of making friends. If you stop thinking of yourself and start thinking of those people around you, you can make more friends in two weeks than you can in two years by trying to get other people interested in you.

The late Alfred Adler, one of psychology's great men, said it quite simply: "It is the individual who is not interested in his fellow men who has the greatest difficulties in life and provides the greatest injury to others. From among such individuals, all human failures spring."

So the first rule for making friends is to pay attention to other people.

The second rule for making people like you is: *smile*.

I know that sounds simple, but you would be surprised at the effect a smile has, both on you and on others. The moment you smile, any bitterness you may feel seems to dissipate itself from within. It has to be a real smile, but if you do smile, it will make you feel good and make everyone around you feel that you are genuinely happy.

The third rule for making friends is to remember names. A girl's name is her most precious possession, and she will be much impressed if you can recall it after one meeting. A man is just as impressed.

The fourth rule is to be a good listener. Encourage others to talk, especially men, and encourage them to talk about the thing that interests them most of all — themselves.

Finally, make others feel important.

If you follow these rules, you cannot help having friends, both women and men.

I realize that having friends, especially of one's own set, is not the ultimate in popularity. A girl can be pretty, courteous, friendly, and still not have dates. In fact, I know one sixteen-year-old girl who had exactly that problem and could not understand why.

Remember one thing: While it is rare for a girl to approach a boy, it *is* permissible. So if there is a boy you like and would like to have a date with, use a little psychology on him.

I suppose you could call the boy to ask him for some legitimate piece of information, but there are much subtler ways of planting the idea of a date in a young man's head.

One way is to plan a party — perhaps a Sadie Hawkins party where the girls ask the boys. Then make it your business to see the boy you want and invite him to the party. It is almost sure to work. And once you have had him at close quarters for a few hours, he'll probably be interested in calling you for a date quite soon. It is a little like feeding a very young kitten. Sometimes you have to dip its nose in the milk first before the kitten gets the idea.

But remember, don't try to trap the boy into a phony party that consists only of you and him. Under those circumstances you will probably never see him again.

Another way to attract a boy is to discover what his hobbies are. A hobby can be cultivated without being obvious. If he collects stamps, for example, start a little collection of your own, and as soon as you know what you are talking about get into a casual discussion that will let him know you have a common interest.

Or if you find that he is a tennis player, there is no law that says you can't turn up on the park courts on Saturday morning. The least that can happen is that you will get some exercise and improve your own tennis game. But if he sees you on the next court, he may just wonder what you look like without your racket.

Perhaps the girls you know are having some kind of outing (if not, plan one) and you can casually mention it to the boy and suggest that maybe he would like to come along.

If the boy is a bit shy, you can take matters into your own hands by indicating interest in something he talks about, like saying: "I've just been dying to see that movie myself." Unless he's absolutely impossible, he should take the cue.

Remember, if a boy asks you to do something you don't know how to do — such as bowling or bicycling — you had better learn fast. Don't try to get him to do something else.

If he suggests that you go to a place that your family has put out of bounds, don't hesitate to tell him so. He will respect you for it. A boy also will respect the curfew your family has set. The same goes for any rules your parents have laid down.

And when he asks you for a date, accept promptly and pleasantly — if you are going to accept. The giggling "maybe" that some girls use always irritates boys. The sooner you answer without fuss and bother, the better you are going to make him feel. Bear in mind, you have made him feel "smooth," and that makes him think you are pretty smooth too — it is a bit of simple psychology that is good to remember.

To be popular with boys — or with men, for that matter — girls and women must exert themselves, and in exerting themselves they bring forth what we call sex appeal.

I don't suppose that anybody knows a real definition of the term "sex appeal," but I can tell you why you find yourself attracted to a certain type of person even though you don't know the reason for it.

Sex appeal is dependent as much on the psychological reaction of the beholder as it is on the charms of its possessor. The tall, dark handsome one and the man with Charles Atlas muscles and the blond crew cut are widely different in appearance and personality and character. But each represents, to some particular woman, the epitome of sex appeal. You might say that sex appeal is very much like an allergy. The effect of allergy is much the same on all victims, but the cause might be chicken feathers or it might be dust. It is an inexpressible thing that has to do with the erotogenic impressions we have received through the senses — seeing, hearing, smelling, tasting, and touching — throughout our formative years.

We get our first adolescent impression of an appealing person through the sense of sight. The things that please us are very different from the things that please someone else. A girl who finds a great deal of sex appeal in a Rex Harrison haircut will be repelled by a chalky, naked Australian bushman. It is all in the way we have been conditioned to certain standards of beauty.

This conditioning has been going on for a long time. It takes place so early that one of the simplest Binet psychological tests at the very earliest level is an aesthetic test. A child is given a picture of a pretty girl and an ugly girl and is asked to tell which is prettier.

Many things contribute to developing one's attitude —

the people we meet, the books we read, and the movies or television heroes and heroines we admire. Western women used to speak with revulsion about the poor Chinese women who had their feet bound. And the women of China would squeeze their tiny feet into tinier slippers to make their feet seem even smaller.

Meanwhile, Western woman, while sneering at the Chinese, was lacing herself into a steel-and-whalebone corset that displaced her interior to the point where she was subject to fainting spells. But she suffered this torture so she could boast that a man could span her waist with one hand. Men considered the woman with the smallest waist to be a prize.

It is a tribute to woman's toughness and ability to stand years of self-mutilation that you and I are here at all. It also shows you what a woman will do to attain that elusive quality known as sex appeal.

There is more to this appeal than fashion, though. A woman may be undeniably beautiful, yet lack what we call sex appeal. Men may grant her perfect beauty, yet find her cold or dull — and merely on the basis of visual impression. That is because the man has a certain taste or preconceived notion, and this is not appealed to in any way by this woman.

Quite often men want some particular imperfection in a woman, perhaps unconsciously. Many men are attracted to near-sighted women. Some find sex appeal only in women who are fat according to present standards. (Those standards have changed remarkably in a century.) Sometimes the deviation from conventional standards of beauty is such that the man seeks actual deformation. Every man has his

41

own concept of sex appeal, as far as external appearance is concerned. Considering the vast variety of human appearance, this is an excellent augury for the survival of the human race, at least. It also permits us as women to indulge in one of our favorite pastimes, trying to figure out what someone sees in someone else.

What makes sex appeal in the eye of a man? A whole flock of things that started when he was a little boy. He may have been fascinated by the sheen of his mother's silk stockings and may have stroked the shining silk and loved its smooth touch. Now here he is a man about town with an eye on the ankles of every girl he sees in the street.

A man seeks the person who in some way expresses his emotional ideal and who, he will say, has sex appeal. Let's say that when he was three years old a certain middle-aged aunt always brought him peppermint drops whenever she came to call. He was a glutton for peppermint drops, and a pleasant experience was associated with the presence of his aunt. The aunt may have had a husky voice — and there goes a tile into the mosaic of his future ideal. And suppose a little later his favorite teacher used a certain type of light perfume. Chances are that later on he will be more pleasantly attracted to a user of a delicate perfume than to one who chooses a sandalwood or musky perfume. Anyway, as time goes on he has acquired a tremendous store of impressions of all kinds. He hasn't thought much about them and he hasn't gone around formulating a special field. But someday he will run across a person who has, for him, the charm of sex appeal. She may not look like much, but the sound of that beautiful, slightly husky voice would move his heart if it were made of stone. And the perfume she uses just sends him into a tailspin. But of all causes for attraction, the most common attraction-link is that the girl in some way physically or psychologically, resembles his mother or possesses some of the traits he identifies with her. This is very apt to be the case unless his childhood environment was one of anxiety and repression — in which case he may choose a girl the diametric opposite of his mother.

That's why a man who vows he can go out only with tall pale blondes often finds himself acquiring high blood pressure over a short plump brunette with a voice that rings a bell somewhere in his unconscious mind. Now, you may ask how this information can help you to have sex appeal for someone else. The answer is that it depends upon the extent to which you anticipate a particular person's ideal or are able to make the most of any qualities you possess that may be termed by someone as sex appeal. There are certain qualities that are generally thought by everyone to be desirable qualities for a person in our culture and in our particular time. Our definition of qualities that are most appealing changes from time to time. Film stars, for example, are chosen to be groomed for stardom because they possess those characteristics which current fashion dictates — qualities that make one sexually attractive because they fulfill certain unconscious needs. For example, the bosom fetish has been related to Philip Wiley's idea of *momism*. Our cultural insecurity makes men want to return en masse to the babyhood symbol — the security of the mother's breast.

I don't have to remind you that a cap of shining well-groomed hair, a glowing clean skin, and an attractive, pleasant disposition are going to rate high with anyone in our culture. And I don't have to remind you that meeting people with similar interests may lead you to someone whose particular ideal qualities you may possess. Your first step is careful personal grooming. After that your best bet is to study the particular make-up of the person upon whom you wish to make a devastating impression. Obviously you can't subject the object of your affections to a psychoanalysis, but you can keep your wits about you in the game of discovering his secret ideal. For example, if he remembers with deep nostalgia the lilacs blooming in the dooryard of his childhood home, you don't have to be a genius to think of using lilac perfume. And this will probably please him very much. If he remembers the little girl in the light blue dress, you might consider wearing this color. You can learn his taste in food and music and take the trouble to indulge him. And then some fine evening when he drops in for dinner, there you are in a pretty blue dress, serving a meal that his mother might have cooked. He probably won't suspect the lilac perfume — all he knows is that you are mighty attractive this evening. And you'll have, in his eyes, sex appeal. You can see that the possibilities are numerous and probably endless. It's entirely up to you.

One of the questions I have been asked many times by girls who want to be popular is what should they do about their own obvious faults? Should they hide them from others, or should they admit them cheerfully or painfully? Or what should they do?

I have a simple, unequivocal answer to that question: Hide your faults every time. Forget them if you can when you are with others. Correct them when you can. But never, never make a public display of what you consider to be your own deficiencies.

I can remember not long ago visiting a woman acquaintance. I had no sooner come in the door and taken off my coat than she began apologizing for the condition of her house. She pointed out that the living room needed painting. She showed me the hole in the wall where her son had pounded a hammer, and said wryly that she had just not gotten around to having it fixed. She emptied an ash tray and explained how sorry she was that she had not gotten around to cleaning the living room before I arrived. Then I did notice a film of dust all over the room. I also noticed that the house was messy. I would not have noticed any of these things if they had not been called to my attention. When I did notice them and when they were made such an important matter, I felt uncomfortable. And it will probably be quite a while before I go to see that acquaintance again.

Without meaning to do so — in fact, in her effort to apologize for her own deficiencies as a housekeeper — she had made herself uncomfortable. She had made me uncomfortable, and our relationship was strained.

It will happen every time. You can be sure of it. If you want to attract a man, for goodness' sake don't tell him all the things that you think are wrong with yourself. In the first place, he may not regard your faults or deficiencies as real faults or deficiencies at all. Remember the odd qualities that can be appealing to a man.

But if you harp on what you consider to be your faults,

45

chances are that he will tend to agree with you — and you will drop sharply in his estimation. More than that, there is nothing more debilitating to your own confidence than a negative attitude. If you start out by apologizing, you may end up by being alone. Nobody wants to listen to somebody else complaining about herself. Don't forget, if the man in question felt as negatively about you as such a performance would indicate, he wouldn't be there at all.

But what about your faults as far as *you* are concerned? Here, do exactly the opposite. Analyze your own faults. Are you neat or sloppy? Are you friendly or caustic? Are you ingenious or tiresome? Do you hold up your own end of the conversation? Where you have faults — and these are usually faults in relationship to your own ideal or to the person in whom you are interested — then work on them. Work on them hard! Master your faults. But do it at home, in the privacy of your family or your own room. Don't inflict your negative attitudes, whatever they may be, on your man.

One of the faults that seems to be quite common among women, one that drives men wild and sometimes drives them away, is tardiness. I know only too well, because I am a victim of that particular fault.

I suspect, in my own case, that my tardiness is a combination of talkativeness and disorganization. Nonetheless, it is a serious personal fault, and unfortunately it is also one that cannot be concealed from a man. That is why I mention it specifically.

I remember when I was living in Balch dormitory at Cornell I was always late for dates. Sometimes I was later

46

than other times, and I could tell often enough that this habit was grating on the boys who came to take me out. Then one time I really got my comeuppance.

It was a winter evening and I had been invited to an informal dance at one of the fraternity houses by a boy I did not know very well. When he was announced from downstairs, I had just gotten out of the shower. I began to hurry, or I thought I did. It must have been fifteen minutes later when someone called from downstairs again and asked if I remembered he was waiting. I did remember, but at that point I was deep in conversation with some of the girls, waving my hairbrush and talking.

Finally I began to rush and got into my coat and went downstairs. The boy was annoyed, I could see, and actually I couldn't blame him. I am sure that unconsciously I was trying to show how important I was, too, by keeping him waiting. As we started for the dance I felt I had overplayed my hand and was very eager to make up for my tardiness. We talked, and his coolness seemed to disappear. When we arrived at the fraternity house I walked into the room set aside for a girls' reception room and began to take off my coat. Then, and only then, I noticed that I was standing there in my blouse, high heels, stockings, and slip. I had rushed so fast at the end that I had completely forgotten to put on a skirt.

Well, what could I do? I wrapped my coat around me, went back to where my date was waiting, and, red as a strawberry, began to explain. This poor, patient young man listened, then took me back to the dormitory so I could get my skirt. But when I reached my room I was too embarrassed to come down. He left, and I never heard from *him* again, you can be sure of that.

Now that I am married I am still inclined to be tardy for appointments — except with my husband. And with him I do my very best to be on time, because he makes such a stew about it. That is quite natural, as he is thoroughly prompt himself and expects me to show him the same courtesy. If I don't, he doesn't like it and he lets me know.

There is one thing you ought to know about tardiness. People who are consistently late are expressing resentments. This may sound strange, but it is true. Like the person who puts off doing things she does not want to do, the person who is always late is expressing rebellion.

This rebellion may have very little to do with the matter at hand. The person who is always late generally comes from a background of strict, stern, authoritarian parents who nagged. Lateness in an adult is a form of revolt against an inner voice that has nagged since childhood.

That is the reason for habitual lateness, but it will not make the habit any more palatable to a man you are interested in just to have him understand it, nor if carried to extremes will it make you popular in the long run.

Being late once in a while is not a crime, and I recommend it as an occasional move for the woman who would be popular. It has a certain test value. If the man is willing to wait for you, he must regard you as valuable. In that sense, planned lateness can be a builder for your ego and that all-important quality — *confidence*.

When I was in college I practiced one trick that built confidence for me and increased my popularity a great deal.

Nearly every Saturday and Sunday I had a breakfast date, a lunch and afternoon date, a dinner and evening date. During the week I didn't date. To make it appear that I had even more dates than I did, I bunched them together.

It would have been simple enough for me to schedule my dates so the boys would not meet. But on purpose I often scheduled them right on the button, so that the boy bringing me home from one date would find the other boy waiting to take me out. My principle was simple enough. I wanted to create a demand by showing the demand. And it worked. I recommend it as a device for increasing your popularity — but only until you find a man you want to hang onto. Then don't try it on him, or you're liable to be back in the middle of the popularity contest once again, looking for another one.

CHAPTER THREE

How Do I Attract a Man?

THERE IS nothing more interesting to a man than a woman who blooms with vitality, vibrancy, and interest in the world around her. There is no woman who is less interesting than the one who slinks apologetically into a room, wearing her inferiority like an ill-fitting dress. Between those two extremes there is a world of difference — and yet the difference between the two is almost entirely a matter of psychology, of attitude.

The very first rule for a woman who wants to attract a man is to put your best face forward. Every time you come into a room full of people make sure you are smiling. If you don't smile well, practice in front of a mirror until you are proud of your smile. Then start trying it out on people. Maybe at first you won't be able to smile well when you are faced with people instead of the mirror. That doesn't make any difference. Even a muffed smile is better than none at all. Keep on trying, and eventually your smile will become natural and spontaneous.

The second rule to attract a man is to dress with a little

bit of dash. Don't wear clothes that are dowdy and dull. That is just like carrying a sign that says: "I Am Just A Dull Girl, Pay No Attention to Me."

Dress in clothes that have both color and attractive, simple cut. Spend a little time — and even a little more money on mistakes — to find out what colors are especially your colors. Then don't be afraid to wear them.

I know an attractive girl who never stood out in a crowd because she would always wear unrelieved grays, navy blues, and blacks rather than the gay, bright colors she could wear so well.

One day when the two of us were shopping she tried on a dress that was fire-engine red. It snapped up her appearance so much that I insisted, over her strong objection, that she buy it.

The end of this story is that she suddenly realized she could and should wear brighter colors. Now she dresses smartly, and just through that change alone she has gained self-confidence and attention. When I see her at parties these days she is always surrounded by a little knot of men.

If you are the type of person who looks better in subdued colors, your accessories should be planned to add dash and interest.

Having attacked the problems of approach and dress, let's talk for a moment about physical deficiencies.

What if you are too tall?

If you have that problem, you are probably inclined to join the foolish Order of Slumpers. These are women who not only slump a little bit but try to cut an inch off their height by flattening their feet in shoes that have no heels.

This makes them look like tall girls with very big feet. Another trick of the slumpers is to hang their heads like tired flowers drooping on the stem. This immediately creates the impression that the girl must have something wrong with her neck. Obviously, to any male in his right senses, there is little appeal in a woman who may soon become a stretcher case.

To get the full impact of a slumper's posture, try it once before a mirror. Is this not what you saw? Your shoulders sagged. Your spine went into an S-curve. Your chest caved in. Your stomach jutted out. Your hips dropped, and your waistline increased an inch or so. Quite definitely you gave the impression of being round-shouldered, flat-chested, large in the derrière, large in the hips, and large in the midriff. It certainly was not a very attractive picture, was it?

The real answer is to take advantage of your tallness. Make a virtue out of what you think is a fault. You will have to be a little tough with yourself here and stop wishful thinking. If a man you are dating thinks you are too tall and this gives him an inferiority feeling, you are not going to conquer him by slumping. So forget about him and those like him and fish for others. You will find them.

Many of today's most beautiful actresses range in the six-foot area. They haven't found that their height has been a handicap. Many of them accentuate their height by wearing extremely high heels and wearing their hair upswept or hats that make them look even taller. I know that many a tall woman has felt that there is no such thing as being too tall as long as you can carry yourself properly. A tall woman may easily be as graceful as a short one.

So my suggestion is: Don't try to conceal your height. Stand tall. Walk freely and easily. To look your best, you must form the habit of standing tall all in one line.

Here are some specific suggestions:

Don't choose completely flat shoes. A little heel, at least, is required. And an intelligently chosen wardrobe can give the impression of less height: full skirts, wide belts, and short boxy jackets. Above all, if you want to look a little shorter than you are, avoid long unbroken lines, vertical stripes, and too long hemlines that accent the distance between head and feet. But again, above all, don't slouch!

There is a hormone therapy that can be undertaken during adolescence if your doctor recommends it. This is a fairly recent development and still in the experimental stage, but positive results have been reported in medical journals.

This process involves administering hormones to tall girls to arrest their growth. It is now possible to predict how tall a child will be through an X-ray examination of the ends of bones. In the case of unusually tall girls, for instance, hormones speed up the closure of the long bones of the body and cut down this rate of growth. If the physician feels it is indicated, a boy who is too short can be helped also. Hormone therapy can slow down the rate of closure of the long bones, thus increasing height.

There are other special problems girls and women confront in making themselves attractive to boys and men. One of these I shall discuss because it affects so many people, particularly adolescents — acne.

Acne is the most prevalent skin disease in the United

States. More than four million people are affected by it each year. About 18 per cent of all adolescents have acne to some extent, and while sometimes it is outgrown with no special treatment, it is hazardous to depend upon this because once acne is well established it can only be disfiguring as well as stubborn.

Although acne is not dangerous to life, it is destructive to personality because of the self-consciousness it engenders in its victims. Future happiness and success often have been irreparably and adversely affected by this skin outbreak. For many years no correlation was thought of between acne and allergies by the medical profession. However, some time ago investigators were impressed by the fact that hay fever, migraine headaches, and asthma were usual in the families of acne victims. Studies revealed that many of the sufferers from acne were also allergic to certain things. In recent years it has also been found that hormone therapy is sometimes helpful.

As is true in many other disabilities, preventive measures would have saved a lot of grief and expense. We know that teen-agers are especially susceptible to acne because of the uproar in their glands at this time of drastic changes. So it is advisable for the teen-agers to take preventive measures. The skin is oilier, and this is conducive to blackheads, which often lead to acne. Long before blackheads appear, they should be discouraged by generous amounts of soap-and-water care.

I don't suggest that I am bringing you any but a small part of the big picture of acne. It is often a more complex and complicated picture. But something can be done about it. Basic treatment involves local measures and attention to diet. By "local measures" I mean careful and gentle washing. However, you also have to see to it that you don't eat too much candy or sweets or other substances that seem to cause more pimples.

The best remedy is soap-and-water cleansings. In most cases ordinary soap will do. Used with lots of water and lots of enthusiasm at least three times a day, will help dry the skin, remove dirt and bacteria and excess oil. If your skin is extremely oily, try an antibacterial soap that contains hexachlorophene or sulphur. This may prove especially beneficial. To make sure that there is no speck of grime on your skin when you begin your face-cleaning routine, a fine, lightweight cold cream is recommended to remove make-up and penetrate just far enough below the surface to loosen and absorb any dirt and cosmetics. Follow the cream with soap and water. Rinse thoroughly, first with hot water and then with cold, and then pat dry with a towel. Remember that the skin is sensitive, so try using a gentle soap for these latherings.

It's extremely important that the skin on your head be kept clean. Your scalp should be cleansed at least once a week, and certainly no less than once every ten days. Dermatologists now generally recognize that the danger is lack of shampooing frequently rather than excessive washing. I recall reading an interview with Mary Martin when she was shampooing her hair often during the run of *South Pacific*. She said that to her surprise her hair had never looked and felt so good. When shampooing, avoid letting the dirty soap and water from your scalp fall on the forehead and neck.

It's a good plan to wrap a large towel around the face and neck to protect these areas.

If soap and water and a diet low in sugar and starch fail to prevent the formation of new blackheads and pimples, then the problem is no longer one exclusively for your care at home. The failure of preventive and remedial home care indicates the advisability of medical attention. The medical treatment will generally include a survey of the physiologic make-up, an exploration of the psychological influences dominating your behavior, and your dietary preferences. It will also investigate the possibility of allergies. Your physician may wish to prescribe active chemicals for application to your ailing skin surface. The immediate results may appear worse than the original ailment. But remember, it is the end result that counts. It's possible, too, that the physician will prescribe or inject certain hormones, depending upon your needs.

One thing to remember is that, as far as acne is concerned, general rules are nonexistent. Each patient is a law unto herself. Sometimes other remedies are prescribed. Bear in mind that if you cannot cure the acne you now have by good washing and careful diet, you should consult a dermatologist. He is the only one well enough qualified to determine what may be the problem in your case. Do not depend upon the advice of friends even though they undoubtedly are well-meaning.

Acne, of course, will present problems that are beyond the purview of this book, except in one sense. No matter *what* special problem you face, remember that the key to friendship and the admiration of men is based on *your con-*

fidence in yourself. So even while you are working to solve your particular problem if you have one, do not bury your head in the sand. There are nonallergic cosmetics that help the skin to heal at the same time that they help cover the blemishes. They are not necessarily the most expensive. Use them so that you know you've done the best you can to make yourself pleasing to the eye, and then forget yourself. If you concentrate on others — what they are feeling and saying — you will discover that they are concentrating on themselves too. The impression they will have is not of a girl with pimply skin but rather that of a warm, interesting, delightful person. Develop your interests. Go places where you will see and be seen. Forget your minor disability. If you forget it, others will forget it too.

I remember a girl I knew in school who was terribly injured in an automobile accident. She lost one eye completely and suffered a terrible wound on one side of her face that paralyzed a nerve. She was in the hospital for several months. When she returned to school, all of us wondered how she was going to act. We knew what had happened. We wondered how it would affect her.

Do you know that she did not seem one bit different in her attitude? Within a week she was back in her old swing of things, as popular as ever. She later went to the hospital for plastic surgery, and the scar and paralysis were dealt with satisfactorily. But the most important thing was that she did not let her affliction conquer her.

Because of our undue emphasis on the well-rounded figure, some girls mistakenly consider flat-chestedness an affliction. The artful use of foam rubber and padding in everything from evening dresses to bathing suits has solved that one. Besides, any woman who worries about flatness these days obviously has not been looking over the magazines of high fashion as much as she might.

Altogether, looks or the lack of them depend on individual taste. Some men like big-chested women, some like small-chested women. Some men like blondes, some like brunettes. Some like tall women, some like short women. As there are millions of men and women, so there are millions of preferences. That's why no woman has a right to feel inferior if she is tall, short, slim, heavy, big-hipped, small-hipped, swan-necked, bull-necked, or even just wears glasses.

Now, the preliminaries having been dispensed with, perhaps you wonder if I can offer any help on *finding* an unattached male. I hope I can.

Your very best place to meet a man is through a church organization. Statistics consistently show that marriages that come about between people who have met through the church have the greatest chance for happiness.

But there are less conventional ways to meet a man.

Buy a camera. Any male camera bug who sees you taking pictures will be convinced, no matter how you do it, that you are doing it the wrong way. You will get a lot of free advice. You might also get a camera bug of your own — male.

Go to night school. But don't take home economics or other courses where you are likely to find too great a preponderance of females. Take engineering or mathematics.

You are not likely to become an engineer, but you might engineer something for yourself.

Buy a trip on one of the charter boats that go out deep-sea fishing if you are in a coastal area. These boats are loaded with men. And every fisherman will be glad to help if you look helpless enough.

Buy a share of stock in a corporation. You will be notified of stockholders' meetings and you can then attend. The men you will meet there are likely to have money, which is no disadvantage. Read the literature of the company, and after you have acquainted yourself with the company's operation, politely draw attention to yourself at a stockholders' meeting by asking questions that will show off your intelligence as well as your business sense.

Stocks are generally sold through a brokerage house, which purchases the stock at the going price, arranges for transfer of title of the stock, and takes care of all the details for a small percentage of the purchase price. If you are not familiar with a brokerage house, one of the officers of your local bank will probably advise you. I'd suggest you drop in to discuss your plan to buy some stock with an officer at your bank anyway. You will be surprised at how nice bank officials generally are. Best of all, the banker might just turn out to be a bachelor.

If you do decide to buy a few shares of stock, you may find that you're becoming interested in the stock market and the whole economic setup. Should this happen, I'd make a further suggestion that you enroll in a night course at one of the universities. A course in money and banking might be very interesting for you, and you might also find it a fine place to get to know a few men. Investment clubs are springing up all around the country like mushrooms. You will be welcomed generally even though your investment is small.

Take up tennis. If you are a golfer, drop that game like a hot potato. Men do not join strange ladies at golf — they play through. On the tennis courts it is a different matter. Tennis costumes are more attractive than golf costumes, too.

Get a job in a department store. A boy I knew during the war traveled all over the world when he joined the navy. He never had a bit of trouble finding a date in any port. His secret was to head immediately for the nearest department store, which he knew would be filled with single young women behind the counters. You can turn that one in reverse. You may not want a sailor, but *all* men have to buy things occasionally. Try to get a job in the men's sock or shirt department. If you get into lingerie, the man you meet is most likely to be already taken.

If you live in a city, move into a building made up of small apartments. Single men, as a rule, do not live in large apartments. Make friends with the elevator man. He can tell you which men are single. If you find one, you can always drop a bag of groceries at his feet and leave the rest to chivalry. But don't drop eggs, or chivalry may be lost. Oranges are best. They are not messy, but it takes forever to pick them up.

Try keeping a dog; walk him frequently in the mornings and evenings. Many friendships have begun with tangled leashes. But in the New York area, at least, be careful. Prostitutes often use this approach, and while you are looking for a man be sure you don't get more than you are bargaining for.

So much for finding a man. After that, what? Having found her quarry, what does an honest girl do about capturing him?

First she has to get his attention.

About the time that you were just learning how to put on lipstick, you were probably first told that nice girls don't chase men. Since then you have probably had it pounded into you that men adore the eternal chase but they like to do the chasing. If you are going after a man, you will find that he is running too — but he will be running the other way.

All this sage advice eventually reduces you to a state where you tend to feel like a hussy if you so much as phone your steady date to find out if a dance is formal or not. Strangely enough, the most disconcerted aspect of the advice is that it is all quite true. Actually, however, there is a happy and ladylike medium between the completely shrinking violet and the rapacious, buttonholing type of female. It's all very well to get your man, but be a little subtle about it. It must be done in such a fashion that there is no doubt in his mind that he is the hunter and you the hunted.

What about using a "line"? I favor it as a way to get smoothly over those awkward moments when you first meet. I used one when I was in high school and college and found it worked. My line, which was not a very subtle one, was for use at dances. In college, particularly, many of the dances were informal, and the boys and girls came separately. The stag line was long, but so was the line of wallflowers around the edges of the dance floor. I used my line to ensure that I would be asked for every dance.

After a young man asked me to dance I would whirl around the floor with him for a few moments, making small talk. Then I would look up, blink my eyes as becomingly as I knew how, and ask him whether he liked dancing. (If he didn't, what was he doing at the dance?) He would mumble something about liking dancing to a degree. I would then smile triumphantly and say, "I knew it. You can always tell."

It worked like a charm. The boys came back again and again.

That line was part of my approach to first impressions. First impressions are important, because although experience shows that we are often wrong in our initial judgment of people, many times if that first impression is unfavorable a man will not try to see the girl again.

Making a good impression isn't a matter of some mysterious charm or luck. It does require some skill, but this skill is something that almost anyone can acquire.

The first step in meeting a man is to use restraint. If you try to be overeager, you are going to drive him away immediately If you want to be careful with new acquaintances, here are a few factors that you ought to bear in mind:

Hint at your accomplishments if you wish, but don't do any more than hint at them. Don't try to impress him at first sight.

Don't monopolize first conversations. At the very least, try to keep it at a fifty-fifty level; that is, make sure that you aren't talking any more than the person you are meeting. In fact, it's far better to let the man talk a lot more. There is nothing more intriguing than good conversation, we all know, but remember that the principle of good conversation is exchange of ideas and not a lecture. So the best way you can pay a new acquaintance a compliment is by listening to him rather than talking.

The second way that you can make a good impression upon meeting someone for the first time is by making sure that you keep the conversation alive. This may sound a little contradictory after what has just been said about being restrained. However, being a good listener doesn't necessarily mean that you must assume a purely passive role.

The chances are pretty good that anyone you are introduced to is going to want to talk about himself, and if you are wise you will let him. But at least for a few minutes the conversation will rest upon you — your interests, your manner of living, your occupation. And so, apart from the fact that you should be brief, the most essential point seems to be that you should be enthusiastic about these things in your own life. Don't simulate enthusiasm — people will think you are very artificial. Even when the conversation tends to drift into stale subjects, try to strike some original note and, if need be, perhaps an even daring one. The unique viewpoint is always more memorable than the sheeplike agreement.

The third factor you must remember is to keep hands off.

63

In other words, don't clutch at your new acquaintance too hard even though he seems to be special. The woman who lavishly offers friendship to a newcomer is immediately suspect. Your new acquaintance is likely to think you are so dull and in such little demand that you have to be constantly on the search for new companions. Characteristically, we all tend to retreat when someone clutches at us. So remember that the friendships you treasure most are those that haven't come or haven't been given too readily — you treasure the ones that you feel you had to earn. When you meet someone you think you'll like, of course show interest — but not too much. You might suggest another meeting, but don't do it too soon or make the meetings too soon. You may offer the hand of friendship, but leave it open just in case the other person doesn't want to take it. In this way, you won't be grasping or clutching. There is the possibility that the invitation will be extended by him before the evening is over.

Finally, you have to be careful not to promise too much. If you want to see him again you are likely to try to oversell yourself, so try to control this tendency to oversell.

In overselling yourself you will face the danger of bragging. Furthermore, you may paint such a glowing picture of the life you lead that he may decide you are out of his class, beyond his reach. And probably the worst thing of all in overselling is that you may simply build up to a subsequent letdown. Therefore, if you promise anything at all, make sure that you promise something you can deliver. If you find yourself exaggerating your background, it's because you haven't analyzed your genuine assets sufficiently. Few of us really have to brag. All we need to do is to discover our truly worthwhile points and highlight them. Treating with your own good points, you are not going to have any trouble living up to them.

First impressions are important because the better first impression you make, the more men you are likely to have about you. The more men, the better your chances of getting married.

There have been a number of sociological and psychological surveys made on married and unmarried women with respect to their dating. One of the most important findings that researchers have made is that women who have married have always done a lot more dating than those who have not married. It seems, therefore, that the wider a field a woman has from which to gather a husband, the better are her chances of getting one.

There are other things that have to be taken into consideration when one looks at an unmarried woman and wonders why she has not married. For instance, does she have the motivation to marry? Does she really want a husband? If the marriage she is most familiar with — that of her parents — was an unhappy one, then the mental image of marriage is not pleasant, resulting in a real fear of getting involved in a marriage of her own. Recent studies have shown that many spinsters have remained so voluntarily; not because of their inability to find a mate, but because their unconscious fears have made them withdraw from social contact with men. Such a woman feels insecure in the company of a man and so avoids dates. Because it would be too painful to admit this even to herself, she rationalizes by convincing herself that she is too superior to the men she meets and none could make her happy.

Another factor is the adaptability of the woman. Once she is dating someone, can she be interested in what interests the man? A woman has to find a common field of interest with the man she hopes to marry. Without this, there is going to be too great a divergence of feeling right at the very base of the relationship. Marriage will probably not result, or if there is a marriage it will founder in the shoals of incompatibility.

A third factor of prime importance is the know-how of the woman. Does she know how to be at ease with the man she is dating? If a woman doesn't react to her date in an easygoing manner, he is going to feel ill at ease and is not likely to seek to continue the relationship.

Just what it takes for a girl to get a man can perhaps be summed up in five easy sentences. Succinctly stated, in my opinion these are the basic rules for winning a husband:

1. You must have enough desire for marriage to make the required effort.

2. You must cultivate both a pleasant appearance and manner to make that important favorable first impression.

3. Develop the self-assurance to be friendly and informal even with casual acquaintances.

4. Subordinate your own emotional needs, even though temporarily, and cater to his, thus making yourself "emotionally indispensable" to him.

5. Be willing to compromise on the matter of the "ideal husband."

Remember that beauty and wit, although desirable, are not the essential keys to unlock the door of marriage.

Often a man, without realizing it, woos and wins a woman as a result of a carefully planned campaign on the part of the woman. Advance planning of military tactics seems hurried and haphazard compared to the campaign strategy of some females. Many of our generals might benefit from a closer study of feminine courtship behavior. From a psychological point of view, there is good reason for this phenomenon.

Women, in their struggle to attain equality with men, now find themselves in a vulnerable position. In spite of the immense strides made by women in recent decades, they are still regarded as inferiors where careers are concerned. At the same time, excellence in housewifely qualities is no longer given the respect it once received. Therefore, women are forced to find other means of self-assurance. Some find it in actual achievement. Others find it in subtle control and domination of the male. Many women have achieved an astonishing facility in this art.

Another fact that enters the picture is the interesting difference in psychological significance between two words that presumably mean the same thing. Although the dictionary will tell you that both "bachelor" and "spinster" mean merely unmarried, the atmosphere that surrounds each word is entirely different. They are poles apart. A bachelor is considered to be a man of independent spirit who has decided to remain unmarried out of free choice. A spinster, the subject of many jokes, is considered a woman nobody wants. It is assumed that she, unlike the bachelor, was anxious to get married but couldn't attract a man. When you call a man a bachelor, you imply that he is eligible and attractive. Call a woman a spinster and it is generally regarded as an unflattering appellation, if not worse. Is it any wonder, therefore, that women often take the initiative in courtship?

There is also the added hazard that man must be allowed to maintain his illusion of masculine dominance. Women therefore have had to develop subtle and disguised techniques, plus some not too subtle when the going gets tough. Let's see how you would act if you were utilizing some of these feminine wiles.

In the approach period you would build yourself up elaborately into a picture designed to meet man's requirements. Whatever the man is interested in becomes a ruling passion with you. Although you may never have previously given them a thought, you now profess a profound interest in the most unusual subjects. If the man is interested in geology, he rapidly discovers that you like nothing better than an afternoon spent looking at rocks. What a coincidence! It just happens to be your favorite diversion.

Perhaps you spend an entire day shopping for a proper wardrobe for that first important date. You rush from counter to counter of your favorite store, buying a dress to bring out the blue of your eyes, carefully matching gloves, worriedly choosing the hat that will reveal your profile most becomingly, until you are exhausted — but satisfied.

The next day your natural gifts get a close going over. There is a manicure, a shampoo, a set, facial — the entire works. Altogether, quite an investment in time and money. Then comes the date. The man beholds this heavenly apparition, serene and lovely, and manages to choke out, "What a pretty dress." To which you might say, "Oh, this? It's nothing. I made it ages ago." You imply casually that he would find you looking like this after two years on a desert island.

You are normally an aggressive, athletic type who can beat your husky brother soundly at tennis. Suddenly and surprisingly, you are helpless and a dub. Though you can normally take apart and put together Brother's sports car, you now make it appear as though you couldn't even turn the key in the lock.

The second phase, the attack period, is designed to keep up his unflagging interest. He has already succumbed to the approach, but there is always the dangerous, always present chance that someone else's approach may be superior. The attack is now launched, and here is some of the strategy you might use.

The idea has been built up and has found general acceptance that the male will lose interest if he is too sure of his quarry. Therefore, you start to play hard to get. At this stage we can often observe the interesting phenomenon of "attack by running away" — allowing the man to chase you until you catch him. You pretend a lack of interest that you do not feel. Having waited by the telephone for several nights, when his call finally comes after what seems an interminable period, you refuse a date, explaining that you are terribly busy. This has the effect, as designed, of wounding the male feeling of superiority and causing the pursuit to become more intense.

Now you reverse your tactics. A subtle indication of special interest in him is in order at this point. Cleopatra was probably not the first woman to say that she dreamed of her man the night before — neither was she the last. That sort of line may be overworked, but it will continue in use just as long as it produces the desired effect — and there is no doubt that it does. Nothing keeps a male on the trail like artful flattery and an expressed interest in him. The campaign may be difficult, but the victory lasts a lifetime.

CHAPTER FOUR

How Do I Choose a Mate?

It is one thing to attract a man, but it is another to be sure you really want him before you decide on marriage.

Once you have passed the initial step in attracting the man and are in a position to make a choice, it is well to be as tough with yourself as you are capable. If your choice is between taking this man or not having one at all, you are probably going to think the choice is easy. As a matter of fact, real life rarely produces a situation where there *ever* really is such a choice — except perhaps on a desert island populated by one man and one woman. And even there how could the woman really be certain of what the next wave might bring?

First let us talk about how not to choose a mate.

Don't choose a man simply because you are sexually attracted to him. I know of one young woman who fell wildly in love with a musician because she found him charmingly vague and completely attractive physically. She was going to marry him; she did live with him as man and wife — and he left her flat.

I know another girl whose life was made even more miserable. When she was eighteen she fell in love with a thirty-eight-year-old man who was not only old enough to be her father but was married and had children. That girl in the course of time was deserted, too, when the man finally decided to go back to his wife and children.

The mistake of my second friend illustrates two points:

1. Don't fall in love with a married man.

2. Don't make the mistake of confusing the father image with mature love.

The first point is obvious. Some years ago there was a song with a line that went, "She got herself a husband, but he wasn't hers." No woman is going to have a fair chance for happiness if she gets a husband who isn't hers. She will always be fighting the family image in the man's mind. If he does divorce his wife and marry her, the divorce itself may come between them, or she may live in constant fear that what happened to the first wife will happen again. Obviously he was susceptible once. Why not twice?

The second point — confusion of the lover and the father — is not an uncommon mistake. Almost all girls feel intimately attracted to their fathers until they reach puberty, and this is a perfectly natural and normal emotion. It is only when the emotion is continued to adulthood that it becomes unhealthy.

It doesn't really make any difference how tall or short a man is, or whether or not others think he is handsome, for that is a matter of personal taste.

There are, however, some matters of overriding importance in considering your swain as a prospective husband.

72

Is he mature emotionally? Does he want to have a family? Does he want to settle down? Is he prepared for the responsibilities as well as the joys of marriage? There are just as much of the one as of the other. These are questions that must be asked and answered.

It is hard to define all the qualities that make a good husband, for a husband who would be good for one woman would be unbearable for another. But here are a few pointers:

Is he honest with you in little things? If not, you may find yourself bewildered, then suspicious, then resentful of his actions after marriage.

Does he expect you to take some responsibility in choosing places for entertainment, in the management of affairs that involve you now? That is a good sign, for it indicates a responsiveness and willingness to share. If, however, he wants you to take *all* responsibility, it indicates immaturity and irresponsibility. If he will let you have none, beware. He may be looking for a door mat rather than a wife.

Is he reasonably punctual? If not, he can cause you hours of worry about his whereabouts. Usually this takes the form of wondering if he was hit by a truck and is lying in some hospital, unknown and unclaimed but it might develop into suspicions about his faithfulness.

Do you feel that he will be stable and that this marriage will last? It is surprising the number of young women who go into marriage without really considering the possibilities of marriage failure. The danger signs are posted for all to see, even before marriage — serious philosophical disagreements about the important things in life, disagreements

73

about children and about religious matters. It is easy enough, in the flush of love, to say that these matters "will work themselves out." These important questions have a nasty habit of bobbing up again and again, even after you think they have been settled. Many a marriage has foundered on the rocks of such disagreement even after it was covered by the sands of physical love.

Another very important point to consider is whether or not there will be enough money for the two of you to live comfortably; whether you can see in the future an improvement in his financial condition to support the family nearly every woman wants.

There is no rule that says money has to be a problem in marriage, but where there is not enough of it, money has a habit of becoming a serious problem. Money problems — as well as sex problems — are the cause of much disagreement among young American couples. Don't underestimate money problems, and don't overestimate the problems of "sexual adjustment" that have sometimes been so highly touted in the past as the main cause of marital trouble.

What about mixed marriages, where religion is either a real or implied issue?

Mixed marriages, in spite of the general feeling to the contrary, can be and are successful, despite the pitfalls that two people face when they go into such a marriage. When two people are mature and know exactly what they are doing, they can overcome the added obstacles presented by the union of two people of different faiths.

Marriages between people of similar background do not start off with so many disadvantages and therefore have

74

much more chance of bringing happiness to the couple.

What about marrying a younger man?

Marriage with a man who is considerably younger — say ten years — can present a serious problem. This depends in each case on personalities and age brackets. If, for example, you are seventy and are planning to marry a man who is sixty, ten years doesn't mean very much. But if you are thirty-five and are planning to marry a man who is twenty-five, it does mean a great deal. Even here the possibility of success in such a marriage depends mainly on the people involved. One extremely successful marriage was that between Frederick William Vanderbilt and his wife, the former Louise Anthony Torrance, in the last century. Vanderbilt was twenty-four years old at the time. His wife was thirty-six. His family was shocked, and all New York predicted a speedy end to the marriage. In spite of the gloomy predictions, it proved to be a happy marriage and lasted until Mrs. Vanderbilt died in 1926 at the age of eighty-two.

Frederick William Vanderbilt was an intensely mature man at the age of twenty-four, probably as mature as some men are at thirty-five, and that is probably the reason for the success of that marriage. As a general rule, psychologists do not recommend marriage between partners of greatly dissimilar ages. The difficulties are too many. Sometimes, however, they can and do work.

As to marriages between persons who are three or four years apart — either way — there is little problem. Let us say that you are a woman considering marriage to a man four years younger than yourself.

75

Four years is not a very large age differential, and certainly if he were four years older than you nothing would be thought about the difference in age. However, some women are very sensitive about marrying a man who is younger than they are. In fact, they are so sensitive about it that even if the age difference is a year or less they shy away from this marriage. Behind their expressed rationale is the feeling that they are in some way less protected and less sheltered by a man who is younger than they.

Since, it is true, as shown by statistics, pure and simple, that men have a slightly shorter life span than women, there is more of a chance of a longer life together where the husband is younger. If a woman marries a man older than herself, since his life span is probably going to be shorter than hers, the chances are that she is going to face some years of widowhood at the far end of her life.

Yet, somehow, it is expected by social convention that a man be older than the woman he weds. Social conventions notwithstanding, the chronological age — within reason — should have nothing to do with whether a man and woman should or should not marry. It is far more important that there be close agreement in other areas — in temperament, in outlook, in emotional maturity, and in other similar factors. These things should be given far more weight than a disparity in age. If I were to try to lay down a rule for age difference, I think that within possibly even a ten-year spread age difference matters far less than differences already mentioned and a factor still unmentioned — a factor so important in choosing a husband that it outweighs all the others. There are two vastly important ingredients in a successful marriage: two people who love each other.

This may sound trite, but so does the idea that you must have boiling water to make good tea. It is a foregone conclusion, and too often people forget all about it. Two people can get married — and too often do — who do not really love each other. They get married very often out of a need for each other, and that need isn't necessarily love.

Successful marriage goes far beyond the two people who marry, even though they are the essential foundation. Successful marriage really reaches into the lives of the future generation: your children and your grandchildren.

Where does a successful marriage begin? It doesn't start with the wedding. Rather it starts somewhere in a neverending circle made up of many parts — childhood experiences and feelings, parents who understand co-operation, learning experiences in youth and adulthood, and attitudes in every area of life.

It includes romance and responsibility, sacrifice, drudgery, and the acceptance of disappointments as well as fundamentally rewarding fulfillments — sexual, social, psychic, emotional, and even material.

Always an essential condition for successful marriage is the growth of the two people who are going to marry, a continually expanding understanding of the needs and feelings of the other, and an increasing ability and willingness to give acceptance of the other, respect for the other, and co-operation to the other.

Those who build successful marriages understand that

people grow and change and realize that no relationship is absolutely set and unimprovable. They learn to love creatively with their mate, with their children, and with their friends as well as all others in their circle. They will not settle for less than marriage can offer.

They therefore make every effort at all times to learn. They observe. They try to understand. They acquire the ability to bend and adjust to all situations so that they can develop relationships that give meaning to life.

In other words, building a successful marriage means living creatively at every stage of life.

Co-operation is the very basis of successful marriage. It is as necessary to marriage as stock is to making soup. Almost all people who want to achieve success in marriage can do so if they are prepared for their task and are willing to accept the responsibilities it entails. It is necessary to know that marriage will include the pleasant as well as the unpleasant, the happy and the unhappy, the hard work and commonplace as well as the ecstasy.

Too much emphasis is placed on the word "happiness," and so many people approach married life expecting one long spree. These people are bound to become disappointed. None of us can endure for very long a life made up of party after party. It would eventually become intolerable. Who can live on a diet of ice cream sodas and cream puffs?

You must also not expect that marriage will change a person's basic personality. Marriage will not work miracles. It will give you no more than what you put into it — it will only return it gift-wrapped.

One extremely important word of warning about choosing the man to marry: Don't expect to make him over. One friend of mine thought she saw a great potential in a man who was not anything before marriage and married expecting to change him. The marriage collapsed shortly. Don't try to make the man of your dreams out of raw material *after* the wedding ceremony. That is like walking in quicksand. You may not realize that it is dangerous until you get into it — and then it is too late. Marriage sometimes works miracles in man, but the odds are against it.

It is much sounder to base marriage on what your prospective mate *is* and not what he might become after marriage.

Some women, for some reason or other, make themselves believe that the mere act of marriage will have a magical effect on a man's personality. But the stubborn fact is, as psychologists know too well, that people's personalities are pretty well jelled by the time they are twenty or twenty-five. It will take more than a year or so of marriage to make any changes of any importance. And if you marry a man hoping to reform him, it is unlikely that you will last long enough to do it.

One male animal you ought to avoid like the plague is the confirmed bachelor. Yes, believe it or not, there is such a creature. The really "confirmed" bachelor is a single man who is at least thirty-eight. If by that time he has not found a woman who is adequate wife material for him, then the probabilities are he will never find her.

His personality may take one of two turns. He may be slow and tense or fast and loose.

The slow and tense type predominates. These men are

uncomfortable with women. They feel inadequate and are withdrawn.

The fast and loose type keeps going from one woman to another because he cannot endure a close, permanent relationship with a girl. Both types got that way because they depended upon their mothers for affection and love, which were never given.

To the casual observer a typical bachelor's mother may seem overprotective and fond, but the bachelor unconsciously knows that his mother has let him down. She has never given him enough love and is actually cold, selfish, and inconsiderate. As a result, he is unwilling to give another woman a chance. This is partly because he keeps his emotions directed toward his mother, waiting for her to be as loving as he feels she should be, and partly because he is hostile toward any woman who shows a desire to become important to him. Reflecting his attitude toward his mother, he feels hostile, suspicious, and is absolutely sure the woman who does love him could never make him happy.

The basic problem with the confirmed bachelor is that he is unable to love because he does not know how. This personality is common to all confirmed bachelors.

All of them suffer from inner tension, and if they are sociable it is never with a woman they might want to marry. All of them avoid the dangers of any serious emotional involvement. The playboy bachelor seeks out women who are far beneath him socially, who pose no threat of permanent alliance, and none of whom he could possibly consider as a potential legal mate. These are the "safe girls" in his terms. With them he can relax and enjoy himself. But with a woman he feels is his equal and who might be marriage material, he will be completely ill at ease.

Such a man, even though he is surrounded by true love, will never know or value it. What makes it worse for the woman who loves him, he will probably be repulsed by her demonstration of love. In words or at least in actions he says to her: "You are not going to trap me."

Even more unfortunate for the woman, the bachelor will take advantage of her. He has never been satisfied that his mother loved him enough and he is never satisfied with the expressions of love that his girl friends give him. You are welcome to decorate his apartment, even sew the curtains. You may cook his meals, wash his clothes, and perform whatever other personal services you wish to volunteer, but he will make it clear that you are doing this to satisfy yourself, not him. He simply refuses to give your tokens of affection any serious meaning. If you do too much for him or treat him too well, he will get nervous about the pampering and simply disappear.

No one can give the bachelor the reassurance he demands. No one can love him enough. As a result, he develops a pattern of "moving on" and says that he is looking for his dream girl. If he is the fast and loose type, he realizes in time that one girl is about the same as another. If he is of the slow and tense type, he will make this assumption without trying one girl after another. Gradually he becomes more devoted to his freedom and to himself.

Here are some of the facts that research has disclosed about the confirmed bachelor: He is loaded with neurotic complexes. He is better off if he does not marry, and if he does marry he is a likely candidate for the divorce court. He is more likely to go into a spin emotionally and mentally than the husband type. Among men who die in their early forties, the ratio of bachelors to married men is two to one against the bachelors. They are prone to alcoholism, accident, and illness. Many of them are hypochondriacs.

Understand, these are all statistical generalizations. There are happy, productive bachelors, just as there are happy spinsters and well-adjusted homosexuals, but these are the exceptions.

Nor are men alone afflicted with this introversion that makes them bad marital risks. Some women in this century of emancipation are not emotionally equipped for marriage. It is right that they should stay unmarried, for they will make very bad marriage partners.

How about yourself? The answer, you will find, lies in your motivations. You need enough sexual desire, enough emotional desire for love, enough willingness to share responsibility, and all the conviction in the world that two people and children are happier in a family unit than is a person living alone.

With most women this is not a problem, for biologically women are made ready for marriage and the responsibilities that marriage implies, as far as family is concerned.

Men are different, and the problem with a man, once you have him interested, is to get him to propose. He may not propose — and actually the old bended-knee routine is almost totally out the window, as much as the old custom of asking a girl's father if he might ask the girl to marry him. It is much more likely that a girl and a man will start going together, keep it up, intensify the relationship, and begin to accept the idea of marriage. They walk down the street looking in jewelry shops, and the woman picks out her silver pattern. The man, perhaps with a trapped feeling, agrees. They walk by a china store and she picks out her Spode or her Royal Dalton or another type. Again, he agrees. She talks about apartments or houses or furniture. Quite soon the assumptions are so general that even he begins to believe that marriage is inevitable.

But what if he does not do these things? Then a woman has to push a bit. This is the period of courtship in which the hound closes in on the fox.

It's important for you to get across the idea that you are going to make a good wife.

Men are by nature marriage-shy, as Dr. Reik points out in *Of Love and Lust*. The problem with them is not so much whether they should marry this girl or that one, but whether they should marry at all.

As long as he is young, a man wants to be free. He does not want to settle down, he does not want a steady job, he does not want a family to worry about.

Marrying, to a man, means giving up his life of adventure. Men are afraid of marriage.

What really makes them afraid is the knowledge that, once they are married, they will have to fulfill their obligations to wife and family. They have been educated to that knowledge. They have seen their own fathers doing just that. And they know that eventually they will have to take their own responsibilities in hand. But they want to delay that moment as long as possible.

The truth is, as Dr. Reik says, that marriage is originally contrary to the instincts of men, that they have to overcome resistance within themselves to marry at all.

After all, in the old American Indian tribes women were bought by the night, week, month, or winter. The Cherokee Indians used to change wives three or four times a year. The Eskimos still offer their wives to friends as a "friendly gesture."

Don't forget that to your man marriage means not only happy union but duty, obligation, responsibility, and even only work and no play sometimes.

Women should comfort men and reassure them that they are capable of doing what will be necessary, that marriage does not mean more responsibility, but *shared* responsibility.

If you, as a woman, really understand what responsibility means to a man — what a weight it is to him — then you should not find it difficult to be constant and sincere in your assurances.

However, that is not the only device you should use to speed his decision.

It's traditional that a man cannot stand the sight of a woman in tears and will do anything to assuage her grief. It may become necessary in this period, if there are indications of insufficient interest, to release the flood of tears. This, however, must be done carefully. Not too much, not too little — just enough to touch the heart and awaken a protective feeling.

Purposeful visits to happily married friends are extremely helpful in showing the man what he is missing. A little well-placed and carefully stimulated kidding by these happily married friends can also help. As marriage becomes a real possibility, the man discovers a side of you that he never noticed before. All of a sudden you show great interest in children, home life, and cooking. He may find himself invited to a well-cooked dinner at home — for the first time. His compliments are accepted with modest pleasure. (He doesn't need to know that Mother helped cook the dinner.)

Finally, there is the "now or never" technique to induce actual proposal. You announce sadly one day that you may have to move to another city or go away on a long trip. It's obvious that there is only one way for the man to keep you with him and that is to marry you. He marries you. And the chase has been successful.

Having become engaged, a woman is almost home in her quest for the happy marriage, but not quite. Still, there is the period of engagement to live through. And that often raises a question, even though it may not be spoken. What about sexual relations before marriage?

The answer is simple:

Don't.

Sex is a tremendously inclusive feature of a person's nature. It involves the whole person in a relationship of rare intimacy and sympathy. Any sexual intercourse, however casual or promiscuous, has lasting results. Any sexual union between physically mature and reasonably intelligent people makes them become as one. They will never be the same for the experience they have shared together, nor will they ever again be apart from each other. Something of each sexual act will necessarily carry over into the one that follows. If you treat the matter of chastity lightly, then you are

85

also treating the meaning of sex and marriage with similar lightness. You do not accept the depths and pervasiveness of the sexual relationship, do not value marriage as a profound and permanent relation between two people in love. If you understand how complete sexual union actually is, and if you cherish marriage as a high and holy calling, you will surely want to be chaste when you marry.

People sometimes say — as I assume you are thinking — "But we are in love. We plan to marry. Is there any reason that we must keep apart until our wedding day?" Apart from the social and psychological reasons — such as the uncomfortable or unpleasant surroundings, the fear of being caught, the fear of pregnancy, the guilt of anticipated disapproval — there is also another reason: that is, you may not marry eventually. No one can ever be sure. Many marriages, firmly planned, have not taken place. Often they do not take place for reasons not anticipated by the two most directly involved and sometimes are canceled for the very reason of the intimacy. The man, even though he was the one who instigated and desired the intimacy, still may resent and feel disillusioned about the woman once the act has been consummated. Some marriages have been canceled right at the doors of the church.

Let's say you decide you cannot wait until you take your vows and then something happens to your marriage plans and the marriage doesn't take place. You will have to carry into any other marriage the irrevocable fact that you were involved in a unity, in a oneness with someone else. It seems more sound, no matter how you look at it, to wait.

Another question arises sometimes about chastity. It

usually comes from the female who has already had pre-marital sexual experience and who senses intuitively that she is committed forever emotionally to her partner by this sexual union. When, however, the marriage she expected does not follow and she marries someone else, there is a tremendous burden of guilt carried into this marriage which passage of time somehow will not efface.

If you are going to stay chaste, then you had better learn how to say no.

Every woman goes through this crisis, and her future may depend on her solution. It seems to me that there are two interlocking questions. First, how can a woman tell a man no without offending him? Second, can a young man and a young woman be friends without physical intimacy?

Before I answer these questions, let's see why the questions arise in the first place. Every woman wants to be admired by the opposite sex. When a man expresses an interest in a woman, she is flattered. There is pleasure and satisfaction in being admired and desired. Actually the first part of acquaintance is based in a large measure on physical attraction. If your physical reaction to a person is negative, you will probably not allow the acquaintance to go much farther.

If you never hit it off physically, you would never find out that you both liked to dance, listen to jazz, or play bridge. Your acquaintance would have stopped at "nothing at first sight." So if you were both eligible and have become acquainted, it is natural for some sex interest to be a part of your relationship.

How intense this interest and desire become depends on

both of you. To some men sex is the intended end of any acquaintance, and any other activity is only a means to this end. Other men who are more mature can enjoy the company of a woman without demanding her physical surrender.

You may unconsciously be to blame for whetting the man's desire for you. You may be flirting with the young man. Do you straighten his tie or lean playfully on his shoulder? Or take his hand in yours and tell his fortune? Do you greet him for a date in a tight, low-cut dress? Do you take long rides with him in his car or spend hours alone with him in your home? This would all prompt his interest in you sexually. You are in effect teasing him when you hint by action or by situation that you are available. If you are allowing stimulating situations to occur and do not want to live up to what they imply, you must eliminate them, and I'm sure you will find it is easier to control the relationship.

Now let's consider this question of whether a man and a woman can be friends on a truly social level. I will admit that this is possible among older, more mature, less available people. But even at courting age, if a man really likes you, he will be sensitive to your feelings and will respect them. Men tend to classify all women with the line, "Will she or won't she?" The girl who becomes identified as a willing receiver of all men's favors is seldom respected by any man. The girl who does not have a fast reputation must expect to be tested by the boys she meets. If she resists all, she rises, not falls, into the most refined classification. She becomes a "doesn't" girl, a "won't" girl. Men respect this virtue and admire the lady for resisting her passion and his. On this level they can form a friendship with promise in it.

Now to the question of how to say no. Say it by your actions and your movements. If you are modest and conservative you will certainly not be advertising your physical qualities or implying that you are on the market.

When the question finally comes, and it undoubtedly will, say no lightly, gracefully, charmingly, but emphatically. The next question will be, "Why not?" There are many honest answers to this: "I don't believe it is right, so I would feel guilty." "I would not care for the secrecy of an affair." "I am very fond of you but do not feel that I am that much in love with you yet." "I believe that sex is an important part of *marriage*."

Those answers should do for a start. I suggest that you make the conversation quick and final. So many young people spend hours and hours discussing the problem after it is solved.

Now for some final suggestions. Try not to become too dependent on any one young man. Build up your social life. Give some parties where you can invite other men and women. Let your friends know that you are interested in meeting other men. There is no sense in isolating yourself and helping to create a situation that would become intolerable.

But suppose you really are falling in love with a man. Should you still say no? My answer to you is: By all means. If you resist him, he may go away in a huff and try to forget you. This will test the attraction you have for him. If

89

he misses his bridge partner or dancing partner enough, he may return and ask you to be his wife. If he does not, it will be better for you that the relationship went no farther than the bridge table and the dance floor. Both are much easier to forget than a bedroom.

If you lose a man that way, you will have lost him on your terms, not on his. And, after all, your terms are the honorable, morally accepted ones.

If you say no, particularly when he is interested — or seems to be — in marriage, you may be jilted, of course. But for all the right reasons. He really wasn't interested, after all.

Being jilted is not at all an uncommon thing. I am sure that a woman's immediate reaction would be one of two things: either to cry her heart out or walk around in a bit of a daze and ask "Why?" over and over again. The questions that go through her mind each time are probably, "How could he do this terrible thing to me?" and "What did I do that made him change his mind?"

What might she have done that made the young man change his mind?

It is possible that she really inveigled him into proposing in the first place. Sociologists say that the present vogue of early marriage in this country is really credited to women rather than men. Girls in their late teens and early twenties so often see their girl friends from high school days getting married and having babies that they feel they want to follow the crowd. They have a fear that perhaps they are going to be left behind —left "on the shelf," so to speak. Many a young girl in this situation often translates a young man's protestations of love into a proposal of marriage. Before he knows it he is involved in buying an engagement ring and selecting a wedding ring to match and deciding on all the other little things that go before marriage — selecting silver and china patterns and looking at furniture. All right as far as it goes.

But perhaps someday he wakes up rather suddenly with the realization that really he isn't ready for marriage. There are probably many things that he has wanted to do, many places he has wanted to go, before he settles down. He realizes, perhaps, that he is not quite able to support a wife in the way he would like and that the prospect of having children is just a bit overwhelming. Not being near the girl he loves, he realizes that he doesn't want to get married at all. So you see, too often young men get inveigled — perhaps "snared" is the better word — into marriage before they are ready.

So remember, it's always best to let the man make up his mind for himself — no matter how much undercover prodding you may do.

Part Two

THE MARRIED WOMAN

CHAPTER FIVE

How Do I Hold My Mate's Love?

THERE ARE certain basic differences in the temperaments of men and women, and marriage is not going to eliminate them. Some people grow up accepting that. However, too many people assume that from the day they are married a man and woman will enjoy the same things, feel the same way, and like the same people. As a matter of fact, people are inclined to put the pressure on to make this happen, and when a husband continues to be completely masculine, some women are irritated, exasperated, or even disillusioned. Both men and women can go into marriage looking for something that isn't there and missing what is: the companionship of opposites, the mutual enjoyment of natures unlike their own.

There is something else that women unconsciously expect that in the nature of things they are not going to get, and that is complete, constant attention. A husband has a lot of things to think about. He must think about succeeding in

95

his job; he must think about paying the bills. He has to think of fixing the carburetor of his car and straightening out his fishing tackle. When you marry you move out of the world in which someone is always there to listen.

Like all human beings, men are many things. They are people who like to crouch in the bitter cold, hidden by rushes and marsh grass, and wait for birds to fly overhead. Or they like to tramp across fields, carrying a gun and annoying rabbits. Some of them like to go out on a golf course and chase a little white ball around all day long. When he can't indulge in sports, the average man reaches for the sports page of the newspaper. And although some of a woman's recreations overlap those of a man's, to most women sports are an occasional pleasure, while to a man they may be almost a necessity. Unless a woman has grown up in a household of brothers, the importance and attention given to sports come as a surprise to a young bride. I know one woman who almost broke up her marriage in the first year when she walked into the living room and at the crucial moment of a championship fight that was being televised asked her husband if he minded if she turned the thing off for a while.

Men are other things too. They are people who are fascinated by power and by engines that create it. They like power in a car. They like to take the lawn mowers apart. They like to watch the mechanic at the garage — and they are likely to be involved in these things often at mealtimes or when some other important chore has to be done, like taking down the screens or putting up the storm windows.

Men, unlike women, are not inclined to be talkative. You

96

can't sit around and chitchat with a man as you do with the girls you lived with. With the right companion — his wife — he might recall in words what happened on the fifth hole when he played golf last Sunday or discuss what was wrong with his drive on the seventeenth. By and large, however, when something is finished a man doesn't want to hash it over.

Men can be deplorably uncritical about people too. They tend to accept people at face value. This can be a rather aggravating trait that can lead to disputes after a party and often can make a woman seem overcritical when she feels that she was merely being discriminating.

Men are friendly and they like their women to be friendly too. They are also reserved, perhaps because of a desire for self-protection. They need to feel free. A woman wants to be the center of family life. On the other hand, a man wants the comfort of a home and the assurance of a basic routine, but he doesn't enjoy the hundred little chores that go into making up a home. Men are peaceful too. Women like to stir a pot and see what is cooking. Men don't. Women like to create some excitement around themselves. Men are amused by these superficial feminine fireworks. At heart, however, a man is a person who feels a need to rely on a calm and predictable state of affairs in his home.

Most men like to keep a good strong rein on financial decisions in the family. This has a sound basis, since a man, under the law, is responsible for the family expenses and knows it. This responsibility is part and parcel of a man's character. Men are also egoists. Now remember that having a strong ego is not to be confused with being selfish or self-centered. It is something in a man that makes him think well enough of himself to stand up to the world with strength and with success. It is a part of his fortitude, and no one relying on any man can afford to overlook the value of a healthy ego or try to batter it down. Tied up to his ego is masculine pride. Of course women have pride too. But a woman's pride is different. A man's pride has many facets. It can be connected with picking up a check in a restaurant or with the way his wife looks when she goes out with him. It may be connected with the ability to get a superficial response from a girl at a party. It may be just owning a new car. It can take forms where a more realistic approach would be sensible — for example, driving in the wrong direction for blocks rather than stopping to ask directions.

Another thing, remember that men are sentimental and that they are vulnerable. A man can be deeply moved by something that will make a woman just raise an eyebrow. However, men don't make an institution of sentiment as women do. As to their vulnerability, we have to remember that men can be so vulnerable that they can be very deeply hurt — even when unintentionally. Children — their own children — can hurt them, and their wives can do irrevocable damage.

When we get married, what we can look for and get is a mutual appreciation of differences in temperament. The equipment called for is not the reforming urge or the low-spirited complaining outlook. It's an understanding heart and the courage to face something new. You may shake your head sometimes over this man you married, but most of the time you will be shaking it in approval.

The most important year of your marriage is the first year. This is the year of decision — the year in which you and your husband will find a foundation for permanent compatibility and happiness, or the year in which tension will break your marriage.

About 25 per cent of the divorces in this country come within the first two years of marriage — often at the end of the first confused and bewildering year. Even if the sick marriage continues beyond this first critical period, a basis for divorce and unhappiness may have been established.

A glamorous and thrilling courtship may end abruptly with demands of a new marriage and the problem of establishing a practical home life. Some couples are unprepared to accept this strange reality. Small difficulties mushroom, and they lead to the divorce court.

Here are nine rules to help newlyweds weather the dangerous first years:

1. Recognize that problems are to be expected as a part of life. It is very important that you realize that you are not the only married couple in the world who have ever had problems during the first year of marriage.

2. Do not try to have exactly the same interests as your husband. You should have some different interests, because this gives marriage some spice.

3. If your sex life is not satisfactory within a year's time, seek competent help from a doctor, a psychologist, a psychiatrist, or a marriage counselor. This is very important. Sex problems somehow do not go away by themselves, and the longer you wait, the more difficult they become to solve.

4. As far as parents are concerned, don't establish any

fixed patterns for visiting them or having them visit you. They should fall in the same category as friends. You will visit them whenever you feel like it and expect visits from them under the same circumstances. These visits should be pleasurable and voluntary and not an onerous duty or obligation.

5. There usually is a problem of finances. Try to work out a budget that is practical and, above all, *stick* to the budget.

6. Budget your time as well. Make sure that you have enough time for pleasure as well as for work, because pleasure is an important part of marital happiness.

7. Your marriage is a partnership.

8. Health is a vital factor in happiness, so make sure that you arrange to see your doctor and your dentist regularly. Be conscious of your physical well-being. You would be surprised to know how much unhappiness stems from unhealthiness.

9. Expect trouble, but also expect happiness. Feel confident that you will be able to face the future and that there will be a happy future for you.

Any couple who can come through the first year of marriage successfully can feel truly that the worst is over. In this first year they have made adjustments, many of which have been painful, but they have also laid the firm foundation for married happiness the rest of their lives, and the two following danger zones — the seventh year of marriage and the period sometime between the fifteenth and twentieth years — will be a lot simpler to face.

One of the truly important matters in holding your husband's love is your ability to make a partnership of your marriage and to carry out your full responsibilities as a partner.

There are many adjustments to be made in marriage. These adjustments come easily if the people involved are emotionally mature. What is implied by "emotional maturity"? This is a term often used when referring to marital problems. "Emotional maturity" means a great many things. It means self-confidence; it means ability to maintain an even temper and to obey the rules of the game cheerfully; it means consideration for others. These are necessary ingredients for successful participation in the intimate personal relationship of a marriage. The mature woman is considerate of the failings and shortcomings of her husband and tries to make a constructive contribution to his development. The mature woman respects the rights and the personality of her husband and is willing to make the compromises necessary to attain a finer relationship. When a problem arises, both parties contribute to its successful solution even though it may involve some mutual sacrifices. Neither party dominates and neither party submits, but both submit to the common cause — namely, success of their joint enterprise, which is the marriage.

"Well," you might say, "in that case why is so much written about the necessity for women to adjust and so little written about the necessity for men to adjust?" Perhaps it is simply because men are out in the business world every day where — if they are to succeed — they learn the necessity and the how-to of adjustment quite naturally. It is as though they are going to a school for emotional adjustment if they are to remain successful in business. On

101

the other hand, the average wife finds herself suddenly thrown into a career — marriage — for which, more often than not, she has no special training. There is no one to whom she has to adjust for a great portion of the day, so she finds it more difficult to make the necessary adjustments when her husband is home in the evening and when children come along later.

This is not true for all women. Certainly women who have spent time in the business world before marriage find that adjusting to the difficulties and problems of marriage comes easier. Neither party to a marriage has the right to expect the other to make all the necessary changes and adjustments. Yet it is all too often true that some women do demand greater bending and yielding on the part of their husbands.

The two areas in which a normal man must dominate in his marriage — if the marriage is to be stable — are the sexual and financial realms. Most men no longer object to their wives working if the husband's job is more responsible and pays more money. They want their wives to be ardent and responsive sexually, if they themselves retain the aggressive role and set the sexual pace.

Some women, however, find it difficult to the point of impossibility to live this way. These women are fundamentally domineering and aggressive types. They are unable to subordinate their own personalities to their husbands'. They are the sort who nag their husbands about the how and when to love. In some cases women such as these rob their men of their sense of masculinity and of their spontaneous feelings of affection by demanding that the husbands perform in the way they — the wives — dictate.

And don't forget your appearance for a moment. Newlywed wives, with honeymoon lingerie and their brand-new pride in marriage, generally take care to be especially attractive when their husbands are home. But after a while a certain familiarity sets in — a comfortable old-shoe attitude. This is very bad news for the romantic side of a marriage.

What man wants to make love to an old shoe?

Do you look like a dream or a nightmare?

There is nothing about cold cream and hairpins that will arouse a man's ardor. So make sure you look attractive. Your most attractive.

Cultivate your inner beauty. This is not an easy job, but its results can assure you satisfaction with yourself and can go far toward cementing a long and happy marriage.

First and foremost, you must be or you must become radiant. This requires a basic joy in living. It requires some sustained enthusiasm and perhaps some sophistication — if you define "sophistication" as not pretense and posing but a happy participation in the life all around you. Perhaps the most important factor in inner beauty is intelligence.

The second factor to remember about internal beauty is that you must be conscious of self, without being self-conscious. Study your good and bad points objectively. Remember that you lose charm when you become self-centered, but beauty is every woman's business and she should improve herself as impersonally as she would perfect

103

any other work of art. An emotionally healthy woman cares about how she looks. As a matter of fact, psychiatrists find that, as a female patient begins to recover, one of the signs of that recovery is an increasing interest in making herself attractive.

Thirdly, remember to keep a good interest balance between yourself and other people, neither too self-centered nor, at the other extreme, too interested in other people to the exclusion of yourself.

Fourth, learn to know and understand love. I don't mean the externals of love such as kissing and hugging and love-making. Love means spiritual depth; it means inner peace. It means that you cherish the people around you and are cherished in turn. This is a matchless combination, and if you do not love — and if you are not loved — you can never be beautiful, no matter what else you do.

Fifth, build a healthy attitude toward beauty itself. You don't have to be Miss America. It's a matter of becoming a beauty queen within the limits of your own potentials. You have to make the most of your own physical assets. And build the best you can on the best you have.

Last, make sure that you do something active for at least several hours a day, and this is aside from just housework. Get outside and walk in the park or get to swim or play tennis. Or do setting-up exercises in your bedroom before an open window.

When I said marriage was a partnership, I meant just that. A partnership survives and thrives only when the partners work at it. One partner may work harder than the other, but both partners work. In the marriage partnership your husband is contributing most of his share by working at his job, supporting you, and making it possible for you to have a home.

That is not the end of his responsibility to the marriage partnership, to be sure. But within the home, the major responsibility for success or failure of your marriage will rest on you — the woman. You cannot escape that truth.

Marriages fail for many reasons, but in failing marriages the same set of reasons crops up time and again. I have found that the tragic stories of lost marriages almost always follow an unhappy pattern.

The first common factor in marital failure is a *hangover from adolescent days*. Emotional problems that are characteristic of adolescence are carried over by some into adulthood. Women of this sort seem to exhibit the emotional instability of teen-agers. It is an instability toward relationships in the social area as well as in the sexual area. In other words, these women really haven't grown up. They may find it difficult to grow up without some guidance.

Another common problem is early conditioning against the idea of marriage. Memories of an unhappy father or mother, of their attitudes toward love and sex, are major influences on a woman's feelings about marriage. If your home was full of warmth and security, if there was a great deal of love, then the chances are that your own marriage will be built on the same pattern. If it wasn't, then you have a clue that there may be trouble brewing in your marriage if you are not careful. Psychologists have discovered that *early conditioning against marriage* is often a major cause of sexual dissatisfactions too. This leads to

105

squabbling, and certainly squabbling leads to a bad situation for the marriage. Its circle is one of those self-perpetuating ones. It's a vicious one.

If your childhood was marked by frequent bitter quarrels between your father and mother, then the little germ of these quarrels may have been passed on to you and to your marriage. And you, unfortunately, will pass it on to your children.

A third factor is lack of confidence. I don't mean to say that you must be a braggart to be a success in a marriage. But you should possess a certain amount of self-confidence and a certain amount of assurance of your worth as a person. I don't think any man wants a meek little mouse for a wife. Low self-opinion usually stems from childhood and adolescence. The fears and anxieties that are created by such a low opinion of oneself can ruin a marriage. It will create doubts in the mind of your husband as to your ability to face the problems of life.

A very frequent problem in marriage is a self-willed flight into rejection. This occurs when the woman reacts to fears of being rejected by assuming an "I'll reject you first" attitude. If a woman is unsure of herself she feels that her husband is going to reject her sooner or later. But she is unwilling to do anything about this and she is unwilling to wait for him to start rejecting her. So unconsciously she begins to reject him first. She complains that he has changed and has become sulky and never pays attention to her. And the difficulty is that this dissatisfaction usually spreads from dissatisfaction of the husband and will carry over to her children. Sometimes it carries over onto parents and friends and even inanimate objects.

Another female problem is a revolt by the woman against the idea of being feminine. Women too often reject the female role in social and marital relationships. That is a characteristic of many career women who have sacrificed their family for monetary or social gain. And some of these women often become serious competitors with their husbands and with other men. Psychologists have found that women who revolt against being wives and mothers usually come from homes where their own mothers exhibited a negative attitude toward sex. Friendships in the formative years of these women were difficult, and feelings of loneliness and inferiority developed therefrom. In marriage, these women usually show a strong distaste for sexual relationships.

The counterpart of this in men is a dissatisfaction with sex and a sort of projection. This is really a case of a pot calling a kettle black. The husband who suffers persistent inadequacy in sexual relationships is often overly critical of his wife, whether or not this criticism is related to the basic problem. Though not always recognized as such, considerable ordinary family bickering grows out of sexual dissatisfaction and projection. Such a simple situation as a wife accusing a husband of being hotheaded and argumentative may be evidence of it. She forgets that it takes two to carry on a quarrel. Of course women can fall into this category as well.

Ego strain is another factor, and this seems to combine

all the pressures of modern living — the marital pressures, the social pressures, the familial pressures, the economic pressures, and even the sexual pressures. Their impact upon the individual shatters the feeling of personal security that either partner in the marriage might have. As ego pressure accumulates and mounts, it's quite human to cover up feelings of insecurity with a show of self-righteousness, and that leads to criticism of others. In today's rapidly moving world the danger of suffering from ego strain is increasing more and more.

Sometimes these factors occur singly; more often they occur in clusters. You can be absolutely sure of coping with these problems only by being born into a harmonious family where your mother and father never quarreled or faced financial problems and were not ashamed of sex. On top of that, you have to be sure that you didn't bicker with your brothers or sisters, that you got along with all your friends in school, that you were given certain honors at school, and finally that you married a paragon who had no faults at all. This is certainly impossible. But we do the best we can.

Remember that most marriages succeed — they do not fail. Marriage is a normal relationship, not abnormal. It is not difficult for normal, well-adjusted human beings to make the relatively minor sacrifices demanded to make marriage succeed. For a woman in particular, there is obviously so much more to be gained in making the sacrifices than in not making them that few women would even argue the point.

As far as sex is concerned, you ought to know a bit about the factors of frequency, desire, and success.

The male's time of greatest sex desire is in his early years, early in his marriage. At this time the female responses are relatively undeveloped. The wife is still struggling with inhibitions that prevent her from participating freely in marital activity. During her formative years she was told that sex was taboo. She was counseled to protect her virginity. She was told that "going too far" was a disastrous sin. Practically, she knew that "getting into trouble" before she was married was a social disaster, so the sex act was strictly taboo. She felt guilty if she even considered premarital intercourse.

Then she was married. Suddenly all of the inhibiting forces are withdrawn, as far as *everyone else* is concerned. But she cannot eliminate them from her mind. She cannot change overnight from a virtuous, self-controlled girl to what the world would have considered a wanton woman twenty-four hours before.

This feeling of guilt and revulsion must gradually erode. Some women can adapt easily and quickly, but others never do. Their psychological inhibitions are so strong that they can never co-operate freely in marital intercourse.

The result is this: The eager, healthy, desirous male is frustrated. She objects to his demands or even his thoughtful requests, and he resents this. At the peak of his desire she is inhibited. Gradually he loses interest, and at the time when she is most desirous he is bitter and resentful. So, if there is a failure or a lack of compatibility, it can be blamed upon the couple's inability to work out their relations during the early years of their marriage — years when, by mutual discussion and a willingness to co-operate, they are able to overcome their disparity more easily than in later years, when habits are more firmly set.

Woman

The average woman reaches her sex peak at the age of twenty-six or so. But in examining the "sex peak" idea there are three *separate peaks* we should discuss.

The *peak of frequency:* the maximum opportunity for intercourse.

Next, the *peak of desire:* the time in life or the age at which the individual feels the greatest need for sex experience.

Finally, the *peak of success* — and this applies to women primarily — the age or time at which the female is most likely to achieve orgasm or have a satisfactory completion of the sex act.

You may not realize it, but the age for each of these three peaks can be quite different, and there is a marked difference between the peak of opportunity, desire, and success in the female and the male.

First, let's look at the peak of frequency of opportunity. Incidentally, my statistics come from the *Kinsey Report* and a number of other scientific studies that corroborate these findings.

The peak of frequency for married couples is highest among healthy, vigorous teen-agers and couples who are in their early twenties. The frequency is generally directed by the young husbands. They are anxious to prove their masculinity. They are at the peak of their physical prime. Regular intimate relations are a new-found freedom, a new liberty for them. So they are at their most persuasive when *the marriage* and *they* are still young.

As a result of male insistence, then, the peak of frequency is in the late teens. At that age the average female is having

110

intimate relations with her husband about three times a week. Some 14 per cent of the women in their late teens are having intercourse seven or eight times a week. At age 30 the average is 2.2 per cent; by 40 the average is 1.5 per cent; by 50 the average is once a week; and by 60 the average is about once every two weeks.

Understand, these figures do not necessarily reflect the *woman's desire* for sex or her *success* in the sexual experience. The wife may, in fact, resent her husband's *desire* and wish he could be satisfied with less frequent intercourse.

This is not to be expected, because the fact is, her husband is at the peak of *his* desire. Maximum responsiveness to sexual desire in the male occurs in the late teens and early twenties.

This need gradually declines from a peak at this time into less desire as the man ages. In middle age, when the man goes through a period of psychological revolt against growing old, there may be an upsurge of sexual desire. This is less a physical need than a psychological urge to prove that his masculinity is not on the decline. Then the object of his desire and the partner of his intercourse may in all likelihood *not* be his wife.

The peak of desire in a female comes later than it does in the male. Her maximum responsiveness is in her late twenties. But unlike the male, the female will maintain this peak of responsiveness at the same level for most of the rest of her life. In other words, her desire will *not* gradually decline.

Although she will reach her peak of desire in the late twenties, her peak of success may come a little later. Only

111

about 70 per cent of the women between 16 and early 20 reach a climax in intercourse. From 30 to 45, almost all of the women — 90 per cent of them — are at least occasionally experiencing the completion of the sex act.

So we see that during the peak of frequency for women the peak of desire and success have not been reached. The time of greatest desire comes later, and the time of greatest success follows that.

If you are frigid, it is probably a matter of psychological inhibition based upon your early training. Some religions, some cultures, some families are particularly strict. If the subject of sex was particularly taboo when you were a young girl, it is logical that you will experience some difficulty in co-operating with your husband fully in sexual intercourse.

Couples who find sexual satisfaction early in their marriages do not necessarily follow the curves of opportunity, desire, and success. They then are not "average" but unusual. This co-operativeness and sense of fulfillment invade all of their marriage activities, and their marriages are not "average" but ideally unusual also. This is the goal of every family.

One of the great assets you have going for you, from the beginning, is that your husband fell in love with you or he would not have married you in the first place. Your job is to keep him that way.

CHAPTER SIX

Making Marriage Stick

MANY JOKES have been made about the "seven-year itch" in marriage. In fact, there was a play on Broadway that dealt with that exact phenomenon, the second period of crisis in every marriage.

Having successfully passed through the adjustment period of the first and even second years, the average marriage proceeds smoothly until it reaches this second crisis. The term "seven-year itch," of course, is a convenient label because statistically this seems to be the time of trouble, though crisis may come in the sixth year or the ninth. But there will be such a period, its degree of importance depending on the marriage.

Marriage, as anything else, has its ups and downs — its good seasons and its bad seasons — its high points and its low points.

Psychologists have found there are three times in the lives of married people when such low points occur. I call them the "three danger zones" of marriage.

The second danger zone is the one commonly called the

"seven-year itch." There is still a third period of trouble, and this comes for the average couple sometime between the fiftieth and twentieth years of marriage.

And what about the "seven-year itch"? This is a "rash" of a different nature. It seems that a sudden need for romance — for adventure and excitement — develops in people after six or seven years of marriage. There is truly no intention of breaking up the marriage, though sometimes discovery of the extramarital byplay leads to broken homes. The husbands or wives who get caught up in this problem are usually quite content to let the whole business be forgotten after a short time. It has satisfied their need to know that they are "wanted," that they still *can* attract another (even though they are "old married persons"). A woman I know who went through this danger zone told me recently: "I just wanted to have one exciting date. It was something I knew would never happen again. I knew very well I would go back home that evening and take up the household routine as though nothing had ever happened." She had no desire to be unfaithful, though unfaithfulness can develop, and often does, in such situations.

The third trouble period is also marked by boredom. A married couple have grown to know each other *so very well,* they virtually have nothing left to say to each other — or so it seems for a time. The marriage appears to be growing into nothing more than a routine companionship. Each know the other's feelings, the other's jokes, the other's reactions.

In every case — in each of the danger zones — the basic answer is sincere consideration of the problem. Don't just

114

become discouraged because you feel your marriage is like a leaf dying on the vine. Be willing to discuss the problem with your spouse; be willing to see a marriage counselor (your minister, priest, or rabbi, or a psychologist) and be willing to put some intensive effort into meeting the challenge.

Nowhere in anyone's life is there anything that can bring so much rich reward as a happy marriage. You have to be willing to work at your marriage, especially when it is in the danger zones.

Because of the boredom quotient that exists in the danger zones, you may find yourself faced with the problem of infidelity. Your husband may become involved in a casual affair or in something more serious. And here you must take yourself in hand to meet the situation.

The fact that a woman is considered attractive doesn't ensure her that her husband will not be unfaithful. In fact, attractiveness of the wife doesn't seem to enter the picture.

I know one couple who were very close. The husband was highly attentive — in fact, displaying many overpossessive signs. One day his wife went to spend the weekend with her mother. She came home earlier than planned and, to her utter surprise, found her husband in the midst of an affair with a neighbor. They had had no previous arguments or disagreements — nothing of that nature.

It was simply this: From her husband's viewpoint, he was punishing her for having "deserted" him to spend the weekend with her mother, a reaction that came out in psychoanalysis. More husbands — and indeed wives — suffer from this emotional immaturity than is realized. And it often accounts for many bizarre reactions that unaccountably take place in marriage. But fortunately few are so drastic.

In all probability you will never have to face up to the problem of infidelity. Happy, well-adjusted husbands are not inclined to slip off onto the primrose path, and if at the point of the "fatuous forties" they feel their manly powers slipping and want to prove themselves still attractive to women, they are usually well enough set in the path of marriage that they will not go so far as to have an affair. A man knows, as well as a woman, that once he has involved himself with another woman sexually, he has passed the mark. His life will be affected in some degree. It will never be the same.

And most men in their forties value home and family and the comfort of good conscience more than any ego satisfaction they might achieve by an outside conquest.

Even if your mate may sometime slip off the marital path, the chances are that you will never hear of it. He will do almost anything to conceal it from you, to maintain his happy home.

If you do learn of your husband's infidelity, the chances are that he wants you to find out, either consciously or unconsciously. There is no need for him to bring home the lipsticked handkerchief — he can easily throw it away, and you would never miss it. If he does bring it home, watch out, for you are being warned that your marriage is in danger. Whether the lipstick represents a casual kiss or an intense affair, the danger is real. He may be punishing you or he may be caught up in a chain of events leading to disaster.

If you have married a promiscuous man, you have a serious problem that can be solved only by adjustment, divorce, or professional assistance for his psychiatric troubles. But what if your husband is not promiscuous and yet has slipped and had an affair with another woman? Should you forgive him?

That is an individual question, one that a woman has to answer for herself. The answer will depend, in part, on the circumstances, on the time of life of the husband, on the age of the children, if any, and on the age of the wife.

It is very easy to say that if your husband is ever unfaithful you will leave him like a shot. But if it does happen, and particularly if you have small children, just how will such action affect your life?

Remember this: Your divorced husband, up to late middle age, has the pick of all women up to his own age, from the age of consent on up. But you, as a divorced woman, must operate in a drastically reduced field, and the older you grow, the smaller grows the field of eligible men. If you have children, the problem of marriageability is greatly increased for you.

So if your husband has been unfaithful and if he has repented and promised not to stray again, my suggestion would be to make up, forgive him, and make the try. You have too much at stake to do otherwise. And most often the woman who tries a second marriage puts far more effort into making it work than she would into trying to keep her first marriage together. After the infidelity, even if he is still involved, the chances are he will return to you.

There are a number of types of women who prey on

117

married men from thirty-five to fifty. This is the royal court of home wreckers — *the ladies in waiting* who surround a husband's throne.

Lady Hurt Herself is a self-destructive girl who delights in hopeless romances. She works herself up into a state of romantic love and expects to be mistress of the castle overnight. This cannot happen, and the agony of delay and frustration are exactly what she wants. She feels the ecstasy of guilt and is exhilarated by the humility of second best. If the situation changes from impossible to possible after months of divorce wrangling, her interest lags. Her unconscious will start to crawfish out of the romance and start her looking for some man who is more completely married and unavailable. If the object of her bruising affection becomes single suddenly, she will run screaming to the nearest self-torture chamber and begin again. This lady in waiting will make your husband's life miserable by complaining about delays and so may achieve the final rejection by sending him back to you.

Lady What's-the-Use knows better than to complain. She knows she doesn't want the man really, only his company and conversation and a few pleasant dinners out. She is a companion more than a matrimonial prospect, although she has no objections to the pleasure of his company in the bedroom. She admires the man's cleverness and stimulating talk much more than his sexual powers, and this will begin to dawn on the man. He may become suspicious about all the giving he gets without any of the typical demands of a wife. He may wonder what she is waiting for and get

118

scared away, or he may wonder why she is so vague and unemotional and be bored away. Either way, she had what she wanted — some company. And marriage being what it is from her experience with dissatisfied husbands, the lady says, "What's the use?" and starts listening for interesting conversation again.

If this type is your hubsand's "new woman," you have a chance of getting him back voluntarily. But look out for her sister . . .

Lady Mother Hater . . . because she is out to get *you* and every other middle-aged woman. She has a feud going with you, because by age and situation you are a blood relative of her mother. There was a fight between them back in her childhood, and the prize was her father. It was a nightmare battle that she keeps fighting over and over again. Her memory of it is so vague that she has even forgotten the prize. Any man who is old enough will do, because the prize is completely unimportant. The enemy — her rival — is the target, with no holds barred. You have never met the girl, never done anything to her, but she hates your type. Her whole mission in life is to destroy the middle-aged wife. And if she dares to try to hang onto her husband and preserve her marriage, the wife is the object of the strongest force of female hatred ever released. Although her motives are infantile, her methods are bitterly adult. She will win — by taking your husband, though she has absolutely no use for him, or by sending him back to you a total wreck.

There are others, but those are the major classes.

Has it struck you that the types of ladies I have described

have no desire for your husband? It's true. He is king in the game, but, as in chess, he is only a pawn — entirely for their own use.

Far more serious than a single misstep by an erring husband is the aggravated problem of the loveless marriage.

Many wives lead miserable lives for years because they get as far as realizing that their marriages are loveless. However, they feel that they cannot take steps to alleviate the situation. There is no cut-and-dried solution to the loveless marriage. But something can be done about the feeling of being trapped.

Loveless marriages fall into three classes. There is the marriage in which love never truly existed for either member of the marriage. There is the marriage in which one member of the marriage loved but the other never really cared. And in the third type both members really loved each other during the courtship and the early years of marriage, but circumstances broke down the relationship and love seemed to die. This last type is the most hopeful, because the trouble is usually a matter of outside pressure.

In a one-sided marriage, where a woman suffers and clings for years to the partner who does not love her, there is always a tendency for her to think that maybe he will change. She thinks that maybe one day her husband will love her again. The unloved partner is less a victim of a loveless marriage than of her own refusal to face facts. It's always better to give up false hopes and work on the real situation. Once having faced the fact, then you can try to do what you can to keep your life interesting and hopeful in spite of it. If a woman is thirty and finds her marriage loveless, she can end it and start again. But if a woman is fifty, she faces life, the rest of her life, alone. Uprooting at this stage of life can do little to bring happiness.

The same holds true when children are involved or when religion forbids divorce. A marriage involving long years of association, or a number of children, or severe financial hardships in the event of divorce — in these cases, salvage is the best answer. Insight, perspective, and patience are often a better answer than divorce in cases of incompatibility. They can mean the start of a new life for the one who felt trapped in a loveless marriage. Telling yourself over and over that you are trapped and doing nothing about your situation can constitute the real trap. It is possible to learn to be self-sustaining within such a marriage.

Psychiatry feels that only when a situation is quite hopeless, when it is affecting your health, when all attempts to remedy it fail, only then have you the right to consider the possibility of terminating that situation. To go on living miserably and unloved with a partner who makes no effort to help matters is futile. Before condemning your marriage as loveless and yourself as trapped, I suggest that you examine your own feelings very carefully. Is the marriage truly loveless? Or is it romance that seems to be lacking? Many women mistake the natural behavior of a man comfortably settled down in harness for lovelessness. Remember that the average husband is no Don Juan or Romeo. In fact, I strongly suspect that even Romeo, given a number of years of marriage, would have become quite an average husband.

There are a number of characteristic behaviors of some

women which contribute to the speedy demise of love. One is bossing or tyrannizing your husband. You may lead him, push him, guide him, help him in any way. But don't boss him. He will grow to hate you for it.

When a woman bosses her husband, he knows it and rebels in chagrin. She knows it and raises her voice in justification. And the world knows it and laughs in amusement.

It may be possible that by bossing you have helped your husband to success in his profession. Judicious prodding and correction in his grammar and selection of his clothes may have helped make him what the world terms a successful man. However, he is too often a wife-made man, a slightly ridiculous creature in his own eyes and in the eyes of those who know him well. He is not a man in his own right; he is, rather, the husband of a certain woman — a domineering woman who enjoys dictating.

Another serious cause of marital upset is female moodiness.

Every one of us has moods — we call them our ups and downs. There are days when we are sad and there are days when we are glad. Such days sometimes run into weeks or, on the other hand, sometimes they are of comparatively short duration. The thing is, however, that most people don't realize that moods really run in cycles.

Mood cycles have a rhythm — a curve that goes up and down. You may not be conscious of these swings of emotion, but they are there. What's more, if you do recognize them, you haven't the faintest notion of what causes them.

Some people don't suffer from their moods. But this riding on the crest of a wave one day and toppling into its trough afterward can be perfectly normal and a frequently encountered situation. It would add to everyone's basic happiness, efficiency, and general adjustment to work — and to life in general — if every one of us was aware of what our emotions are up to and when they are about to play us tricks. They say that to be forewarned is to be forearmed. The real danger is not the fact that we have mood cycles but that they sneak up on us and take us unawares.

It is most unfortunate when the up-and-down curves of a married couple are practically identical. When down, they quarrel and don't speak. They are both irritable. They eat together in silence and sleep in separate rooms, or they may even go so far as to take trips as far away from each other as possible. A short vacation apart can be beneficial to a married couple. They say that absence makes the heart grow fonder, but not when the absence is motivated by a downswing in mood. Then bitterness — even hatred — may enter the heart. Many divorces come about that way.

One is likely to suspect the potential troubles that may flare up when both husband and wife are in a pessimistic mood at the same time, yet feel that everything should be just fine when each of them is feeling high. This is not true, however. Here, too, there is danger, but of a different sort. It is during such a temporary exuberance of spirit that couples will spend a lot of money unnecessarily. They may suddenly buy a new car or take an expensive cruise or pledge themselves to pay a sum to some community project that they can't afford. They do something in an extravagant manner by which their desires are allowed to override their prudence and reason and common sense. It's also under such overconfident influences that a man, upon the advice of his wife, will tell his boss off and quit his job. Or the wife, at the suggestion of the husband, will take their savings out of the bank and splurge on a mink coat.

These swings of emotion up and down can cause a lot of trouble. Yet they are inevitable and perfectly natural.

Worry does not help your mood cycles. But there are things that you can do to bring them under the control of your will.

The first thing to do is to make a chart. On this, mark your mood swings in such a way as to show graphically how many days you are optimistic and how many pessimistic. Also, the chart should show whether the swings, one way or the other, start gradually or abruptly. The chart will also reveal to you how often you have an upturn of feeling and how often a downswing. In this way you can tell ahead of time which days or weeks, or even months, will be your elated or depressed days. And so you will be able to prepare yourself not to fall overboard because of one or the other. Little by little you will be able to chart your own course and experiment a little. Find out when your emotional curve is most beneficial for clear and straight thinking — it may be on an upswing or it may be on a downswing. It will also help you to realize that when you are down in the dumps you are going to feel better in a few days. Besides, when you are well acquainted with your own mood cycles you will never be taken by surprise and wonder what sort of calamity has struck you, perhaps fearing that something has gone wrong with your mind. Even the bad days have an advantage in that the good ones are enjoyed so much more by contrast.

It's a popular notion that women, being more emotional than men, are the only ones who are moody. You can usually count upon women being so at and during the monthly cycle and during the menopause. However, aside from that, both sexes experience mood cycles that are of the non-physiological nature, and their intensity seems to be about the same for both men and women. Of course the intensity depends upon the emotional make-up of the person. The cause of mood cycles — what brings them on — is not known. Lots of things have been suspected, including the glands and other parts of the body, but nothing has yet been proved. You might think that a shock or disappointment or failure might start at downswing and that unexpected good luck might start an upswing. But this is not the case. Mood cycles arise spontaneously, and it's still a scientific puzzle as to why.

Women are far more fortunate in one physiological respect than men; they are able to release all their emotional tension with a good cry, and a good cry can save a marriage from going on the rocks.

It's one of the best forms of emotional relief that you can get. When it comes to tears, women know how much pressure can be removed by crying. A man will have emotion built up within him until there is a lump in his throat that hurts. But what he doesn't realize is that what he cannot put into words he can remove with tears.

You shouldn't be ashamed to express your feelings by

crying. Giving your emotions a fling once in a while does a great deal of good. It removes tension and soothes nerves.

Everybody has to exercise intellectual control — will power — throughout the day. The man in business, the factory worker at his machine, the mother with her children, the teacher at school, the student at his lessons — all of us hold attention to the task. We seldom can express disapproval for fear of reprimand or of losing a job; we must pretend and mask our real feelings so as to remain social beings and not offend. We may be forced to hold back a rising tide of feeling — anger, fear, amusement — simply because the desire for self-preservation as well as our educational and cultural background demands that we refrain from expressing what we really feel. These things demand that we hold ourselves in check.

Nonetheless, a certain degree of emotional draining off is a desirable thing every day in our lives. It helps offset the intellectual control that we exercise continuously.

Tears are not the only means we have of expressing our feelings. There are other valves for our emotions. While people may differ markedly one from the other in possessions or intelligence or social advantages or achievements, they differ only in degrees when it comes to basic feelings. Love and tenderness and sympathy and laughter and tears — all of these and many other emotional traits are common denominators to everybody. The only person who is devoid of emotion is the kind that a psychiatrist would call a psychopath. However, such people are quite rare. We all feel in the same general terms. We all respond about alike to any situation calling for emotional reaction. The only real difference among us is that one person may respond more strongly than another. If we didn't respond similarly, there would be no music or literature, no poetry or sculpture, no painting, simply because there would be no useful purpose to be served by any of these arts. All of us have plenty of feeling; the trouble is that too few of us know how and when to let it loose.

What are some of the other ways that you can gain emotional relief for yourself? Why not laugh — or at least smile — several times a day? Develop your sense of humor. Always strive to see the funny side of life. Attend comedies and farces. Read books that are humorous. And if you suffer from morning grouch, make faces at yourself in the bathroom mirror.

Why not listen to music? It's easy to have a portable radio with you at all times. Or, while you're around the house, a record player, so you can hear your favorites whenever you wish. Play the kind of music that stirs your feelings most effectively. But don't listen to only one kind of music. Get variety into your emotional experiences by switching from popular music to classical pieces, then to lively marching tunes, then to the blues and singing and other kinds of music.

Why not dance and, if possible, why not sing? Get started, no matter how silly or awkward or shy you feel. Once you learn how, you can dance and sing yourself out of almost any case of the blues. In fact, these means nowadays are being employed regularly in institutions to help people with mental and emotional problems toward cure.

Another way is to make as many social contacts as you

127

can. The more people you meet, the more you'll turn your feelings out instead of in. In such relationships you must try not to be too serious. Indulge in gossip and witty repartee. If you do not like some people, keep seeing them anyway. Frequently changing emotional reactions not only improve your personality but keep you out of the rut of boredom and discouragement.

Another good way of releasing emotional tensions is to attend competitive sports where you will want to take sides and yell and become excited — for no better reason, perhaps, than that the rest of the spectators are doing the same thing. Go with your husband to baseball or football or basketball games or tennis matches or the horse races. Go to sports where large masses of people are congregated. These are the best kinds to release the emotions. If possible, try competing in games yourself. Whatever you do, however, let yourself go, and if you can follow the game only over the radio, shut your room door and shout away just as though you were present at the field itself.

Try reading literature and seeing plays in the theater and on the screen that are emotional. Don't always stick to intellectual material. A good western will help keep you *young*.

Above all, in marriage, don't suppress your emotions. Some people suppress their emotions systematically, often through a mistaken notion that their expression means lack of self-control. These people are working with a tremendous handicap. If such suppression is carried on over the years, it may well contribute to the development of neurotic fears, obsessions, compulsions, and other symptoms. Then the proper releases can be effected only through some deeply probing method of analytic psychology.

Making a marriage work, as I have said earlier, is *work*. There is nothing easy about it. A woman's responsibility in this is really greater than a man's, in a way, but if she has not been stripped of her femininity by upbringing or circumstances she is better able to cope with the emotional problems of securing the marital partnership than is a man. Emotionally, women are constructed like reeds — it is natural for us to bend with the wind, bend rather than break. In our elasticity lies the secret of successful marriage.

CHAPTER SEVEN

How to Quarrel Successfully

WOMEN ARE fortunate because they have an open emotional nature — far more than men. They can cry more easily, as noted earlier: laughter comes easy for them — and they can also lose their tempers just as can men. Perhaps that is why they have fewer heart attacks and strokes than men do.

There are times when a burst of old-fashioned temper can be the safety valve to save your emotional balance. There are times when an explosion, featuring all the exasperating things you are thinking or feeling, is the quickest and best way to rid yourself of dangerous tension. But the hardest lesson for the hotheaded individual to learn is *when* to give way and when to hold oneself in leash. The completely uninhibited woman who goes through life expressing herself — no matter at whose expense, no matter at what cost — may enjoy the benefits of such expression, but she also faces the evils that result from lack of self-control.

This woman doesn't spend much time thinking about the possible consequences of her acts. She plunges wholeheartedly into whatever enterprise catches her fancy. And if the

130

results are not what she expected, her anger explodes all over anyone unfortunate enough to be in the way.

At the opposite end of the emotional scale stands the man or woman who is outwardly serene, even in the face of tremendously exasperating conditions. This person is often the one who suffers most from the tension brought on by constantly suppressing his emotion. Such a person has been brought up by very cold, distant parents and spends his formative years in an emotional icebox. Since he didn't see any demonstrations of affection from his parents or relatives, he didn't learn how to express his own emotions. He is drilled in rigid self-control. He is taught that the most important thing in the world is to keep his dignity and to hold his temper at all times. When he matures, this training makes it difficult — if not impossible — for him to unburden his griefs or to draw comfort from someone else's understanding. He doesn't usually have any way of getting outside his shell and turning his own grief to use by trying to help others who may be in trouble.

Such a rigidly controlled person doesn't have the value of the release of self-expression and has to take the long way around when it comes to ridding himself of nervous tension. An argument with a co-worker, for instance, may worry him for weeks, long after it has been forgotten by his momentary opponent. Anger, denied expression, mounts in him and damages him before he can release it. It can cause digestive disturbances — even actual illness. And a long series of tension-making instances may result in a mental or physical breakdown.

Fortunately most men and women do not fall into either

of these two classifications. We are inhibited in certain respects, but we are hotheads in others. For example, some of us lose all sense of proportion and all self-control when the subject of politics is introduced. We may be model citizens and the most considerate of spouses, but let any rash soul dare to criticize our favorite candidate, and watch us blow up.

Others have the best intentions in the world but simply fly off the handle at the slightest provocation. If you belong in this group and really want to do something about that terrible temper of yours, try this:

List all of your emotional explosions during the week, no matter how ridiculous they may appear now that you have cooled down. When you read this list over, you will discover that you have been wasting on trifling matters an emotion that might better have been expended on something more deserving.

Millions of people are ill fed and ill housed. Others are persecuted because of the color of their skin or because of their religion. And you have been working yourself into a rage because a bureau drawer refuses to budge or because your puppy chewed up your shoelaces.

A glance down your list will convince you that you have squandered your emotional energy. You have lumped the little things along with the big and have given each one an equal importance as far as your reaction to it is concerned. Aside from the fact that continuous explosions of anger tend to make you ridiculous in the opinion of your acquaintances, there is the danger that you will lose your own sense of proportion in your ability to distinguish between the

132

important and the unimportant causes of the anger you have been expressing so freely.

Besides, repetition tends to dull the effect of your temper performance. You may make a tremendous impression on your hearers the first time you let loose with a full blast of fury. But keep it up and everyone will soon be saying, "Well, he's off again."

If you treat your temper as an emotional reserve, to be called upon when a fitting occasion demands it, not only will you have more respect for yourself, but you will also gain more respectful attention from other people. Learn to overlook the small irritations.

Shaking your fist and turning blue in the face are of no help whatsoever.

Don't let fatigue ruin your temper, either. You should take time out before you reach such a point of fatigue. When you are tired, drop your work for a few minutes, walk around the block or look out of the window or go for a drink of water. Do anything to give yourself a little period of relaxation. The next time you begin having symptoms of anger make an effort to direct that energy into something more useful. Instead of having a temper fit, seek the cause of the incident that has made you furious.

Make yourself a solemn promise never to lose your temper until you have examined all angles of the irritating situation, with the intention of finding a solution. If you keep that promise, you will find that in nine cases out of ten your anger will have disappeared completely long before you have either solved your problem or decided that it isn't worth the bother.

133

The triggering causes of most temper tantrums are really quite trivial. The truth is that you may have had a number of minor unpleasantnesses, and the effect of each has piled up on top of the others until finally you are just spoiling for trouble.

A politician once told me that one of the secrets of political success was never to lose your temper *by accident,* and never to quarrel with anyone except on purpose.

In other words, as he put it, both losing your temper and quarreling can be useful personal tools in shaping your place in our society, if you use them correctly.

Some family arguments are not only inevitable, they serve a definite and useful purpose in holding marriage together.

Men often claim that their wives are much too often inclined to nag for no reason whatsoever, and the result, the men say, is that their own nerves become frazzled. But there are times when all of us cannot get along with our marriage partners simply because of differences in points of view, upbringing, and values. Even twins, identical in heredity, have their moments of disagreement.

For all of us there must be a way of working this out of our systems. One way is to nag and quarrel. Another is to keep silent and let the irritation smolder. Then we pout.

A pouter can be very hard to live with. The pouter moves around encased in a little cloud of personal suffering. She wants to be a martyr. She adopts an attitude of martyrdom at the drop of a dirty look, and this pregnant silence that she carries around the house really speaks much louder than words. She literally drips disapproval from her cloud.

I think that every family needs to have a little spat once

in a while. It's much easier to live with someone who makes an honest complaint about something than with a self-righteous Pollyanna sort who is so smug and good that everyone seems to feel wicked in comparison.

Nothing clears the atmosphere like one or the other member of a marriage saying how he feels.

However, let me add that this should not be an everyday occurrence. There should be long intervals between these air clearings. Certainly a dozen stormy scenes a year won't do any harm. And these little outbursts are good, not only for the mother of the family, but for the father and the children as well. For the father and children it means that they discover, or rediscover, that the mother, the slave of the household, has some spunk. It may remind them that she has rights and realizes it and means to demand these rights and enforce them.

When you suppress anger, it can grow into a lifetime grudge. And such grudges can destroy family trust and family love.

Home should be a reasonably peaceful place, yet an occasional storm is needed, if only to emphasize that the peace that comes between these storms is wonderful. The tensions of the outside world are such that a home should be a place where you feel you can be completely natural, and the expression of anger has a way of refreshing you so that you can face the outside tensions with the proper perspective. Marriage can be intolerable unless a couple lets off emotional steam once in a while.

Quarreling, in other words, has a certain therapeutic value. But this is true only when quarreling is (1) justified by real differences in points of view, and (2) not carried to the lengths that life in the household becomes one long battle.

The most frequent involuntary quarrels — and very dangerous ones to marriage — are quarrels over money.

Friction arising from conflicting money attitudes is common. Next to sexual incompatibility, the marital issue couples mention most often to psychiatrists is money. The American Association of Marriage Counselors has found that the dominating reason for divorce is money rather than "the other woman." While all types of families are affected, surveys show that most of the money-wrangling couples are in their twenties or early thirties, married from three to ten years. Among newlyweds, almost invariably the first real tiff is sparked by money.

Let's take some specific factors. Perhaps your husband doesn't tell you how much he earns. Obviously that's unfair. One of the cardinal rules for harmony in marriage is that both wife and husband should know the exact family income and the regular expenses. Then they should agree on where the surplus should go. Certainly they should save, but only in a way best suited to both — not so much that they can't enjoy life. As a family, you are "in business," where common arithmetic is essential. You've got to have a definite, realistic money plan and know in advance just how each month's bills are to be paid before you incur them. You need a budget.

What if your husband accuses you of being a poor manager? Is it true? Maybe you've overextended yourself on credit buying, falling for tempting traps such as "easy terms"

136

and "just charge it." Today two out of three American families have a large part of their income committed to buy-now-pay-later obligations. If you've gone over your head, remember that economists say installment payments shouldn't take more than 20 per cent of your income.

But deeper and more subtle factors than poor money handling are involved in family friction. Most of the time it isn't a shortage of money or how it's used that triggers a spat. A man and wife who get along reasonably well may have differences over money, but they usually work out their disagreements without any deep bitterness.

Too often what's actually responsible is some emotional dissatisfaction so hidden in the back alleys of the mind that neither husband nor wife recognize it. A money problem, so easy to pick on, becomes the bone of contention.

If, for example, you don't get up to make his breakfast, he may pinpoint a quarrel on a petty money matter rather than admit he's annoyed at having to prepare his own breakfast. Or you may resent his spending too much time at poker with the boys. The dispute, however, may break out over whether you can afford to go to the theater again or whether you should spend some money on a weekend trip. You see, it's easier to accept the fact that you're angry with your mate for being tight than to admit you're upset for a reason you don't care to put into words.

Thus, you may not be arguing over finances in the sense of cold hard cash. It is money as a symbol — standing for unhappiness, grievances, frustrations, or failure in the outside world. To certain neurotic husbands, money may be an unconscious symbol of masculinity and power. A wife's

137

retaliation against this high-handed money behavior may take the form of deliberately spending money wastefully to express her resentment, or she may choose to punish him in another area of the marriage by failing to meet his sexual needs.

We each have different attitudes that make up a distinct "money personality." There are money neurotics who pinch every penny and those who spend wildly. Some people feel guilty when they spend money on themselves; others hate to part with it for anyone else. There are the compulsive gambler or speculator and the woman determined to keep up with the Joneses. What makes one personality different from another? It all goes back to how you were raised and what money meant to your parents.

If you and your husband have opposing money personalities — let's say he is the hoarder and you're inclined to be a free spender — that doesn't mean your marriage is falling apart. Both of you have to be willing to admit and understand that differences in money attitudes do exist and that you can do something about them. Quietly and reasonably, talk it over at a time when there is no flare-up. Bring your real complaints out in the open. Are you fighting over money or over something that has to do with your feelings about each other? Try to reach a compromise in which you'll both find satisfaction. If possible, work out a common money personality for your family, then choose a way of life to fit it.

There is no single right way to handle money. One couple may be happy when the husband takes charge of the checkbook and accounts; another couple will find it best for the wife, who's more skilled at it, to take on the job; a third will find it practicable to be "democratic," having a joint checking account. Choose the plan best suited to you and don't let people tell you to do it "their way" instead.

If you realize that too much impulsive buying on credit is creating family rifts, consider closing out all charge accounts and going on a cash basis. Some couples cut down irresponsible spending by requiring all checks to be signed by both partners.

Since family life can't be maintained without money, it is natural to think of money problems as the cause of most marital troubles. But you and your husband can usually adjust to any temporary financial difficulty. It's mutual respect and love, rather than money, that keep a couple together.

Quite aside from financial matters, there are a number of reasons for family quarrels. Let us call these matters fuel for quarrels. One type is the "evergreen."

The term "evergreen" is used by writers to describe a plot or a subject that always has created interest and always will. I suppose the most famous one is "man bites dog."

Applying this "evergreen" idea to quarrels, we have: man flirts with blonde neighbor; man makes wife a golf widow; husband gambles away grocery money; husband refuses to help around house. These are all "evergreens." Unfaithfulness in various degrees, neglect, overspending, lack of co-operation, all have been "evergreen" fuel for quarrels since the origin of family life.

You should examine the material of your quarrels to see if they are of this "evergreen" class, and also to see if the same problem recurs. Once you have identified the fuel that keeps blazing up into a quarrel, then you can decide how to eliminate it.

A second type of fuel for quarrels is envy. Without realizing it, many wives, especially women who have worked in offices before their marriage, envy their husbands' professions. They brood over the fact that their husbands get to go to nice comfortable offices and talk to interesting people while they must stay at home doing menial work and spend the day talking baby talk.

This conflict creates so much hostility in some women that they are ready to bean their husbands with a frying pan the moment they step in the front door. They resent what they call "man's freedom." This type of woman feels her husband does not show her enough attention or love because he is distracted or rewarded in other ways. The envious woman who cannot find satisfaction in being a wife and mother may be inclined to quarrel with her husband constantly in order to get even. She will make his life miserable, make him suffer as much as she thinks she does.

The way to avoid or eliminate this fuel for quarreling is for the wife to find greater satisfaction in marriage. If she cannot do this, she can at least realize that her husband's professional life is not as pleasant as she thinks. Most men find enough frustration at work. They hardly deserve an equal amount of hostility and quarreling at home.

A third type of fuel for quarreling, which may be motivated as unconsciously as envy, is sex, which will be discussed in detail in a later chapter. Here let me note only that if a husband and wife are improperly adjusted in their sex lives, they may quarrel constantly.

140

Gradually a constant hostility will invade the marriage. Under these circumstances couples quarrel about anything and everything. Here the subject of the quarrel is almost completely unrelated to the reason for the quarrel. If you are aware that this problem exists in your marriage, you can *stop* trying to settle the argument and *start* trying to settle the cause.

A vital quality in marriage is "forgiveness." When one partner is angry and starts an argument, it is usually better for the other partner to forgive, simply by saying: "I know you believe what you say and you may be right, but we're too angry to discuss it now. Let's forget it until we have the time and the patience to sit down and talk it through." Chances are the subject will never come up again, and if it does and conditions are right, it can be dealt with logically.

Once you're able to classify the fuel of your quarrels, you can probably find the unconscious motivation for them.

As a final thought, and I believe this is very important, realize that when you quarrel you are showing that you care. In some marriage relationships the "what's the use?" attitude becomes so strong that the couple never quarrel. Each simply goes along not caring what the other thinks, what the other feels, what the other wants. In this climate of cold thoughtlessness a quarrel can never occur. Both marriage partners are withdrawn and calloused. They are actually paying no attention to each other.

But while there is enough aggression and interest to draw sparks, the partners still have a chance to work out their difficulties.

Marriage, after all, yields a harvest that is directly related

141

to your planting and cultivating. You *will* have quarrels in your marriage, for all married people either have quarrels or they are involved in loveless marriage.

There are some ways, however, that a woman can keep quarreling down to a minimum and make sure her marriage is as happy as it ought to be.

Here are ten resolutions for you to contemplate:

1. I will always try to look like a work of art — not a worn-out antique. (A man responds more to the sight of a woman than does a woman to a man. Dr. Kinsey has found that men are more sexually responsive to psychological stimuli; i.e., the sight of the beloved woman.)

2. I will show a helpful interest in my husband's work but not try to take over. I know that helping him in his work is like helping someone learn to ice-skate: he won't do well if you push, he won't do well if you pull, but he will do very well if you skate alongside, providing support when it is needed.

3. I will frequently tell my husband that I love him. When the children come, as soon as they can communicate I will tell them how proud we are of Daddy. I know that the children will repeat this to Daddy, and there is nothing like a compliment carried to Dad by his adored and adoring kids.

4. I will make all of the policies on bringing up our future children with my husband, out of the children's hearing. I will not reverse my husband's decisions in front of the children.

5. I will plan for the future and help my husband to plan, so that when we retire we will be retiring *to* life, not from it.

6. I will take pride in my ability to be economical in running the household and the important work I do as a housewife. I will keep in mind the fact that if I were paid at the going rate for all the jobs I do I would be worth over $175 a week. (I had six friends keep a two-week record of the time spent at various tasks. Per week, they averaged two hours as accountant, two hours as secretary, three hours as gardener, four hours as comparison shopper, five hours as chauffeur, seven hours as seamstress, ten hours as cleaning woman, ten hours over laundry, thirty hours in general housework and cooking, thirty-three hours as nursemaid to children or sickroom nurse for husband and children. Multiplied by the prevailing hourly rates of pay for these jobs, as reported in the *AFL-CIO News*, this made each wife worth more than $175 a week.)

7. I will be pleasant and agreeable to live with most of the time. I will take my aggressions out on inanimate objects. (It helps greatly to let off steam. Painting, scrubbing the house, or beating the rugs are wonderful ways of getting rid of tensions without taking them out on someone.)

8. I will make my home a place of comfort for the family, not keep it a showplace for company only.

9. I know that I set the tone for my family's ambitions and interest. I will find one new interest this year.

10. I will treat my in-laws as friends.

It would be pretty hard for a man to quarrel with a woman who carried out all these resolutions all the time. If you carry them out half the time, you will have no real problems with quarreling in *your* family.

CHAPTER EIGHT

Marriage and Personality
(Yours and His)

THERE ARE a great many things for young people to learn when they marry, and most of them hinge on the ability of both partners to adjust to the personality of the person they have married.

You are not going to have the same freedom when you are married that you had when you were single — this should be obvious to every woman. But no woman would marry if the compensations for the loss of freedom were not great. In marriage a woman has the security and companionship that come from sharing life with someone who really cares. Decisions are easier to make when there are two of you to make them. Failures are easier to take when there is someone to share the disappointment.

Yet it continually amazes me to see how many women take partners for life and yet seem to forget that they will have to make sacrifices of their own rights, privileges, and self-indulgences. I do not expect any woman to give up all her rights and privileges, of course — nor does any man in his right mind expect his wife to become a chattel. But time and again marriages have failed because one partner or the other has refused to give and has insisted on being a taker. And because the responsibility for pliability in marriage seems to fall more heavily on the woman, if she is intractable her marriage has even less chance of success than it will have if her husband is stubborn and willful.

Your first responsibility as a wife is to realize that *there will be great changes*. Then the best approach is to try to make the changes best conform to your way of doing things and your husband's way of doing things.

Newlyweds have to establish predictable household routines and schedules. In other words, you have to regularize your life. You have to accept the status of the community of being married and to achieve a feeling that you belong in the married set. Work out a mutually acceptable mode of earning and spending family income. Work out ways of expressing differences with your husband and learning to live comfortably with such differences.

Remember those three danger periods of marriage — the first year, the seventh year, and a period sometime between the fifteenth and twentieth years.

When you marry you leave your home and establish new routines. Occasionally, if the partners have come from very different backgrounds, the routine of the husband and that of the wife clash in the new home. Each tries to enforce his own pattern of living. Then the differences meet head on.

There are many false expectations that people build up as to the way in which their marriage is going to function.

It is natural to anticipate what future events will be like, but many of the expectations regarding marriage are often very selfish. When the married state in actuality doesn't offer all we childishly hope for, we may feel immense disappointment. Too many people get ideas about what marriage is to be like from songs, movies, and television, and sometimes from cheap fiction. These are very far from reality. Then there is the shock of taking on new economic burdens. There are shocks that come with the realization that all problems do not work themselves out after you are married. They will not work out — you must work them out. Differences should be settled during the engagement period, not left waiting until after the marriage.

The business girl turned wife can be a jump ahead of her stay-at-home sisters. A good wife, if she has ever worked, understands her husband's job and is able to appreciate it. She knows that arriving home at five-thirty or six or six-thirty after a day's work means not only being tired but often feeling barely concealed grumpiness. And she realizes that this is definitely not the time to ask whether a new hat will fit into the family budget. Rest, quiet, and peace mean a great deal to a man at the end of a working day. The business girl will realize this because these things often meant the same to her.

Most men have obligations that are part of their job. A wife who has worked in an office is capable of handling this business-social situation and understands how useful she can be in her husband's work. This is a part of the partnership of marriage when a wife with a business background doesn't always cry petulantly that her husband never has

146

time for personal social activities. Instead she is willing and ready to help him meet his responsibilities.

The girl who has been in business is more likely also to be interested in activities outside her home. I have noticed that she is often better informed than her stay-at-home sisters. She had to be if she wanted to get ahead in the office. Business is exacting and competititve. It becomes a question of either learning and maturing or falling by the wayside. And the qualities of a successful businesswoman are not unrelated to the qualities of a well-adjusted wife.

One of the things that office experience teaches is efficient planning. If a girl does not learn that lesson, she can rarely be successful either as a businesswoman or a housewife. The business world is a good proving ground for efficient work methods. A well-run household is a planned household — it is not by accident that it runs smoothly, but because foresight and ingenuity are used in planning a day's work, to say nothing of elbow grease to carry out the plans.

The housewife who budgets carefully has probably had business training. Who budgets more carefully than a self-supporting business girl? Experience in business can also teach a girl how to get the best value for her money. Many other habits can profitably be transferred to the home from the office. A wife can learn how to set up a filing system for insurance records and receipts and recipes. And with such a system nothing ever seems to go astray in the household. The greatest assets in the business world are ideas and the ability to follow through on them. Many women have found their jobs a training ground for developing their imagination and ingenuity. Frequently a brilliant imagination is actually the result of careful analysis of the latent possibility of a situation. The acquisition of this habit of individual analysis can make a wife wonderfully resourceful in all phases of home life, from interior decoration to personal relationships.

And since experience enriches our lives, I think that the girl who has never worked and never supported herself has missed something important. Work should be not only a means of earning money but also an education. What is it that makes business training a valuable asset to managing a household? Simply the business girl's attitude. If a girl considers her job merely an interim period before she finds a husband, no amount of business experience is likely to teach her anything. If she persists in thinking of her office as a kind of reformatory in which she slaves five days a week until marriage pardons her, she is not only mistaken but unwise. The ability to meet people, social adjustment, punctuality, tact, handling money sensibly — all qualities that make marriage happier and more secure — can be learned in the business world. But a girl must be willing to learn. Her attitude and her desire to profit by experience make the difference between success and failure — not only in the business world, but also in marriage.

This does not mean that *every* girl who has worked can do better than a girl who goes directly into marriage without business experience. If a woman has intelligence, a love for homemaking, and a desire to be a good wife, these can be the determining factors.

The truly important matter in marriage, from your point of view as a woman, is that you must want your marriage to succeed enough to *make* it succeed. And this demands a great deal of adjustment, whether you have been a business girl or have lived always within the shelter of your family.

Once you are married, you must become all things to your husband: cook, maid, laundress, baby nurse, cleaning woman, shopper, to name a few of the specialized activities. These are all manual, menial, unimaginative duties from a husband's point of view. As an employee you are expected to have rough hands, stringy hair, and an aching back.

But when he takes you out, your hands are expected to be white velvet, your hair glinting and curled, and your back straight and bare. Your entire appearance must deny the fact that you cook his breakfast every morning. Your gaiety, glamour, and sparkle must deny the fact that your daily companions are infants and animals. You are expected to laugh at jokes you have heard a hundred times and encourage strangers to believe that your husband is a *bon vivant*. You are duty bound to be clinging and submissive so the world will know at a glance that you are entirely his. On the other hand, if you refuse to circulate and demand attention you are accused of being possessive and will quickly find yourself coaxing your husband out of a corner where he has been sulking.

These are all the symptoms that indicate the male attitude in social situations. It is quite different from a woman's. Let's confine ourselves to a party where the couple are among friends. The wife is wearing a festive dress and her husband his best suit. One of her major concerns is how they look together. To many women the highest possible compliment is: "They are an attractive couple."

149

The husband is less concerned about appearance. He wants to give the impression: "They are a unified couple. They are a team; they think alike, have the same ambitions, work and play alike and in perfect agreement, are completely satisfying to each other." The man will undoubtedly want to be the quarterback and call every signal, but with him the ideal impression is: "We are Mr. and Mrs. against the world."

The wife can completely destroy this illusion if she heckles her husband when they are among friends. Unfortunately many women are experts at husband-depreciation. They interrupt his jokes. They correct his version of a family story. They air some petty disagreement they had years ago. And none of this is in the team spirit.

Some wives at a party act as if they had been waiting for an audience to take revenge on their husbands. Others seem to have waited until they found a crowd in which to lose their husbands. These women will latch onto a good listener and bare their souls. The subject may be social, political, or highly personal, just as long as it roots the listener's attention on them. Again the team spirit is violated. The husband drags her away and hisses: "What are you trying to prove with that guy?"

I can almost hear some women fussing and saying: "It's just the opposite with my husband. We go to a party and he leaves me flat. I won't see him for hours, and he doesn't care where I am or what I am doing." This is true of husbands who expect their wives to be independent and on their own. But even the most carefree husband who is at all interested in his mate is nearly omnipresent. He keeps a careful eye on her wherever she goes. Let her start for the garden, and he is suddenly at the door with his arms spread wide and his eyes ablaze. If she begins to act single, he becomes righteously, indignantly married. If she forgets for a moment that she is part of the team and emancipates herself in public, she is going to have to spend a lot more of her time in private.

However, life is not all parties or romance.

For a happy marriage I recommend a simple formula for women — ask less and give more. In other words, love more, think more, and do more. Too many women marry and retire to a semiconscious, apathetic, phlegmatic state. Marriage is like paddling a canoe in deep water. To keep out of danger, you have to keep moving.

Love your husband. Give him his dream woman. Finding a man isn't too tough, but keeping him satisfied can be. When you search your heart and find how little you have given, only then have you begun to love. Be a hundred different women for his hundred different moods, but with one constant heart. It was Rembrandt who once said of his wife that since he had the love of one woman he had the love of all because her secrets were inexhaustible. This is the kind of woman you have to be.

Don't dwell on mistakes that he makes. Be feminine but not female. Keep learning. Make him feel that he is protecting you and at the same time is protected by you against the outside world — that your affection is a buffer for his ego. His failures hurt less if he knows you are on his side.

Don't bore him. Don't freeze into a mold because you think he should like you just as you are. Before you were

151

married each glance was provocative. Keep them that way. Women are, after all, born actresses. It's a shame to waste so much talent. Try being Brigitte Bardot on Monday, Juliet on Tuesday, and perhaps Dante's Beatrice on Wednesday. And remember to stay young in spirit always. Savor every moment of your marriage. That will keep you young in spirit.

One of the worst things a woman can do is expect too much of a husband. Of course no man is perfect, but don't try to play Pygmalion. You can't change a man by nagging and yelling. The only way to change him is by loving. Love will work more changes than all the words in the dictionary.

CHAPTER NINE

Marriage and Sex

WHAT PART does sex play in marriage?

It plays such an important part that it radiates into all other marital areas.

Young women today are certainly more adequately prepared with knowledge of sex than their grandmothers were. However, sex education still falls short of the desirable. A couple of generations ago, if an unmarried girl knew how intercourse was accomplished she was thought to have had a rather liberal sex education. Whether this information had been imparted to her or not, she usually was told in no uncertain terms that intercourse was a cross that women had to bear. She was advised earnestly to submit to her husband, but the implication — if not the specific statement — was that it would be distasteful to her.

Nowadays, with a more liberal attitude with respect to sex education, that onus has been removed from the marital bed as far as the wife's part is concerned. The wife can guiltlessly view her future relations with her husband, not with distaste, but rather with a sense of pleasure and fulfill-

153

ment. It's true that there is a great deal to married life besides sexual relations. But those relations are the basis of
marriage — both in its fulfillment through children and in a
stronger physical and spiritual union of man and wife.
Furthermore, it has been observed that many of the inevitable difficulties of life are handled easily by couples whose
sexual relationship is joyous and meaningful. The same difficulties are magnified to the point of wrecking the home by
couples who are sexually ill adjusted. For those who start
off with a basic adjustment which they owe to their early
emotional development, happiness may come without much
conscious thought about sex. The relationship is so mutually
satisfactory that it seems to take care of itself. One of the
rewards of true love is that it removes the necessity for
talking a great deal about sexual satisfaction.

Those women who have been less fortunate in their upbringing and emotional development need not despair.
There is not so much to what is called the art of love that
it requires superlative talents. A basic understanding of sex
itself, a desire to give full satisfaction to the partner while
achieving it oneself, and an adult love for that partner are
the equipment of great lovers.

One of the most common questions I am asked about sex
and marriage relates to the frequency of normal marital
relations. "Normal" might mean once a month or seven
times a week — or more or less.

Married couples should have intercourse as often or as
seldom as they like. They must bear in mind that it has to
be the choice of both. Sometimes people ask their doctors
what is normal. The answer is almost as vague. The studies

made by Indiana University researchers, which were certainly the most ambitious studies of sexual behavior ever made, showed frequencies that varied, with approximately three times a week as the average frequency. For men the frequency reaches a peak in their late teens and for women in their late twenties. These findings, discussed in an earlier chapter, are invaluable to the student of sexual behavior; for the individual seeking a guide to personal conduct they are not much help — after all, the individual is a person, not a statistic. As for frequency of intercourse and its effect on health, physicians have found that there is no connection.

Another question I am often asked is: Should wives take the initiative in sex? There is no categorical answer. Whether or not the wife should make sexual approaches to her husband depends upon their natures and the frankness they have developed in their relationship. Ideally, there should be nothing they do not feel free to express to each other. But the fact is that some husbands think their wives regard them as lacking in potency if the wives do not wait for them to give the first indications of desire, whereas other husbands welcome their wives' initiative as an indication of love and a positive belief in their prowess.

Even the happiest and most ardent marriages will occasionally come to a time when one or the other member of the marriage is just not in the mood to be made love to. If they are really in love with each other and are mature and well suited to each other, neither member will object to an occasional refusal with the reason stated — that is, fatigue, feeling ill, or whatever.

One reason for difficulty is connected with the reproduction cycle itself — and that is pre-menstrual tension — a problem of thousands of women and one that only recently has become generally recognized for what it is.

In the last generation or more we have seen a big change in attitude toward the beginning of the menstrual period. This is a very significant time in the life of a young woman. It marks the change from childhood to womanhood. In the past it was generally a grim and bewildering initiation because the girl was unprepared for menstruation and was suddenly confronted with it. A girl becomes a woman unlike a boy becomes a man. Frequently there is a certain ceremony of celebration that accompanies the boy's growing into manhood. However, among some peoples, the girl found the sudden appearance of womanhood to be a rather frightening thing. In certain cultures, for example, when a girl began to menstruate her mother slapped her face and then said significantly, "Now you are a woman." Menstruation, the transition from girlhood to womanhood, was not usually a joyous occasion.

It was treated as something that made life rather more hazardous for the girl. And the fantasies of the girl in her puberty helped to magnify the fear and the difficulties of this change. Even in the pre-puberty period her thoughts on such matters were really filled with all sorts of folklore and insinuations and old wives' tales and whisperings. These undoubtedly tended to produce much anxiety and preoccupation with this mysterious occurrence. It was supposed to bring to an end the carefree life of the child.

The attitudes of mothers and their watchfulness and worry at this approaching event had a very marked effect on their daughters, and this effect was quite contagious. A mother's anxiety often left a permanent emotional mark. For the next ten or twelve years, while the girl still remained unmarried, the tension about herself and about her sexual role in life was undoubtedly heightened. In other words, when these attitudes were fostered at the beginning, they became worse.

Most girls, from their pre-adolescence on through to their marriage, have been conditioned to overconcern themselves about this function of menstruation. You can't expect something that is so strongly conditioned in you to disappear automatically. Conditioned reactions have to be replaced by reconditioning.

Drugs have been discovered in the last five or ten years that do help women with the tensions and depressions of the pre-menstrual days. They are quite harmless and they do give a lift to the spirits of many women who take these drugs. They prevent pre-menstrual depression and are also combined with a mild sedative which relieves tension.

Many doctors will tell you that pre-menstrual tension is actually not illness but health, since its occurrence gives proof that the genital organs are performing their tasks. Tensions and strain may be merely an exaggeration of the normal process. These disturbances, in great or small degree, bring a week to ten days of assorted miseries to nearly half the female population in this country.

Physical disturbances are as varied as emotional ones — backaches, headaches, nausea, arthritic pains, nasal congestion, increase in body weight. That's the physiological side of the picture. Psychologically, just as hormones act on the

157

emotions, the emotions also act on the hormones. Whatever a woman is — her strengths, weaknesses, conflicts — all help determine her pre-menstrual behavior pattern.

Only a doctor can prescribe the proper amount or kind of drug, according to each patient's need. In the woman who is at peace with herself and her world, the interplay of hormones and emotion will cause very little upheaval. The pre-menstrual period to her is like any other phase of her existence. Unfortunately far too many women still rebel against being women.

But pre-menstrual tension, while often a cause of many problems in marriage, is not the most common or the most serious cause of differences over sex between women and their husbands.

Of the thousands of excuses women and sometimes men use to avoid sex, the three most common are: it is late, I am tired, the children will hear.

Another evasion is to have a quarrel just before bedtime. There are a thousand excuses. But most of them are simple evasions and do not even come close to the real reason why the marriage partner is rejected.

Many women have told me: "To my husband, sex is nothing more than a physical urge. He can be mean and angry all day, disgusted with marriage, angry with the kids, critical of me. But just the minute the news goes off the television set, he is madly in love with me, or at least in love with making love. This kind of sudden switch doesn't work with me. If he would only show me some affection during the day, I might be able to love him at night."

When husbands complain to me that their wives are

completely cold in bed, I am inclined to ask them how warm they are at breakfast.

Yet I believe that many men are not callous and intentionally mean, but simply put sex out of their minds because they were taught in childhood that the subject was sinful. If they were punished and made to feel guilty for childhood sex curiosity or experiment, these feelings may last into their adult lives. During the day, then, when they are able to concentrate on other things, they may intellectually avoid any attitude of love or sex. Only in the evening when they allow themselves to feel tenderness and passion are they able to recover from the guilt and reveal their desires.

I am, in a way, making excuses for men who are objective in the daytime and affectionate at night.

As a woman, if your husband acts this way — and you can discuss such matters with him — tell him exactly what he is doing. Point out to him that, while a man is easily aroused by the thought of intercourse, a woman is not. A woman simply requires more preparation. She needs verbal as well as physical caresses. She needs to be told in many ways that she is both desirable and desired.

And yet when you talk to your husband be certain that you are doing so with a proper end in view and that you are not simply indulging yourself and justifying your own frigidity.

And the causes of frigidity?

Perhaps the fastest-developing, widest-spreading cause is aggressive reluctance. The wife resents her feminine role in the sex relationship. She has usually learned her mother's attitude of contempt for men and develops a habit of belittling men to weaken them. Her marriage partner receives the same treatment, and unconsciously she does everything she can to make him feel less confident of himself. At the first sign of sexual weakness she pounces on this moment of frailty and thereby increases the probability of its recurring. He may begin to doubt himself and may be finally persuaded into impotence. This provides the woman with the excuse she has unconsciously desired, the excuse that allows her to avoid the feminine role in sex.

Or there is vanity reluctance, in which the woman is so in love with herself that she cannot offer herself fully. She is so preoccupied with herself during the sexual act that she is unable to co-operate enough to make her husband believe he is capable of satisfying her.

Also, there is the problem of failure reluctance. Lack of success makes a woman wish to avoid further chances of failure.

Finally, there are all of the practical conflicts that include fear of pregnancy and all of the minor distractions of worry over unpaid bills, real worry that the children might hear, that someone might see or hear, and even the distraction of wind in the trees. Any of these minor difficulties can distract a woman's concentration during intercourse.

Women should enjoy the sexual relationship in marriage as much as men.

I have often been asked whether a woman is compelled to sleep with her husband just because he supports her. This is an odd and difficult question to answer. By law, of course, there is no such thing in marriage as rape. In other words, the law recognizes the so-called conjugal rights of the husband, and by that I mean that the husband has the right to have his wife share the marriage bed in every way, including sexually. However, in a good marriage the husband and wife realize that sex is mutual and that the satisfaction acquired therefrom should be acquired mutually. Both partners in the marriage are seeking happiness and both are working toward that happiness. And this goes for the sexual side of marriage as well as for every other aspect of marriage. Therefore, for your husband to demand that you share his bed with him is a fair demand. But it should be tempered by the idea that the sharing must be mutually agreeable.

Frigidity in men — and this is not as uncommon as you might think — may end in temporary or permanent impotence, which is nothing more or less than complete inability to perform the sexual act.

The man who is unable to function at all often finds the explanation for his problem in latent anxiety. To explain this condition, it is necessary to mention some other factors that may cause this anxiety. In children, for example, who have severely enforced toilet training there is a latent anxiety about the loss of control that is involved in evacuation. As adults they may never be aware of it, but they are in just the same anxiety situation. For example, when a well-adjusted person is confined to bed because of illness, he may be unable to use a bedpan voluntarily simply because the prohibition against evacuation while in bed is too strongly ingrained.

Similarly, the mechanism that is involved in the physical status required for sexual relations suffers in certain persons

161

from a similar latent anxiety. This mechanism will not respond to their will. To them, the sexual act is a prohibited and anxiety-provoking act. So while a man may desire sex, his unconscious is frightened and retreats from the forbidden. This is what impotence usually consists of. In psychotherapy, impotent men give evidence of this unconscious conditioning. There are childhood fantasies of castration, of guilt, of horrible punishment. These fears — latent in the unconscious — are severe enough to overpower the patient when the mechanism of the body attempts to reach out toward what is prohibited by the deep-rooted feelings.

In cases of impotence it is best to consult the family physician, who will probably send you as well as your husband to a psychiatrist or psychologist, who can give very real help in this area.

One common misunderstanding among women in particular concerns the sexual longevity of married couples. By that I mean the number of years during which intercourse is normal.

Many women believe that sex ends for them when the menopause begins. Nothing could be farther from the truth.

A woman can make a serious mistake by thinking that the menopause brings with it the end of marital impulses or needs. The superstition is, however, widespread among women that menopause closes a chapter of their lives, and many women deliberately stop all sexual activity, leaving their husbands to face the problem of their own continuing needs.

Menopause has no other physical effect than what its name implies. It means the stopping of the monthly occurrence of menstruation. All this means is that the ovaries have ceased to send out an ovum every month, and the result is that the woman is no longer capable of bearing a child. Thus, even if marital desire were only a physical quality, arising solely from the activities of the genital glands, it would not be affected by change of life.

Love, of course, is not a purely physical quality. It is not even largely physical, being much more spiritual and mental in nature. It is a product of all our previous learning and emotions. This is especially true with regard to a woman who has been living a normal married life. In such a case, the emotional habits which give rise to her desires need not be affected at all by the menopause. Of course change of life in women also has many emotional and mental effects, besides physical ones. So it is possible that the emotional desires might be affected. In some cases, women have actually lost all their emotional drive.

On the other hand, some women have found that their needs increase after menopause.

In other words, what a woman expects to happen is likely to happen, simply because she expects it. It is not the normal result or the regular rule for a woman's feelings and desire to be changed. Women should not expect to lose their emotional wants. Very often it is just this pessimism, this mental conviction that they are going to be frigid from now on, which destroys the very powers they would really like to keep.

Perhaps after the menopause the frequency of sexual union will be less. But the main thing is that for these women sex should continue, and they should expect it to continue for many years to come.

Sex problems, of course, are both delicate and urgent. No couple will find it easy to remain together happily if they do not achieve a satisfactory sexual adjustment — and by adjustment I mean simply if they do not really come to an understanding of the needs of one another and an acceptance of the role each must play to fulfill the needs of the other.

A sick marriage needs treatment as much as does a sick person, and this is particularly true when the trouble involves sex, or seems to involve sexual adjustment. Here the professional psychologist, psychiatrist, or marriage counselor can help mend a sick marriage.

A marriage can't be left in a garage for a mechanic to fix up the dents or to change the battery or put in new spark plugs while you go ahead and take in a movie for two or three hours. Everyone must work hard and together to obtain results or even a diagnosis when it comes to problems of marriage.

How does this counseling help?

A marriage counselor does not start by telling you what to do. He listens while you talk out your problem and its origins. He suggests and guides you. He reinforces your understanding and your ability to evaluate. He helps you see the problem clearly, and he helps you to act objectively. He doesn't condemn you or your husband for whatever has gone on. He never never reveals your story to anyone. And he may give you reading material and suggest means of arriving at plans for the future.

People consult counselors for reasons that range from

budgetary problems to those of the in-laws, or sometimes they range in other areas — from the problem of religion to problems of perhaps severe crime. The real reason, of course, is not always the one given the counselor at the first conference. However, before long people who consult with a marriage counselor arrive at the basic reason for their disturbance. They learn to face this problem, and from that point on they plan constructive therapy with the help and the trained and experienced supervision of the marriage counselor. Once you can realize the all-out tremendous effort that is necessary, you will find that you will get help and rather quickly. You learn to understand the problem in its basic aspects and you learn to help yourself. Above all, you will find peace of mind.

We are certainly aware that a mutually satisfactory sex relationship is one of the most important factors that contribute to the happiness of one's marriage. However, sexual happiness just does not depend solely upon sex gratification. Conflicts may exist in other areas that will make the marriage unsuccessful, and this lack of success will show itself in many ways, sex being one of them.

Since sexual union is the most intimately co-operative activity of marriage, the partners have a tendency to come together less frequently and less satisfactorily if there are problems that exist between them. And while the place of sex in marriage is often exaggerated, the contribution it makes to successful marriage is nevertheless important. Certainly few marriages would take place were it not for sexual attraction between the partners. But the personality traits that each partner takes into marriage will have much

165

to do with the degree of sexual happiness that can be reached.

People who are co-operative, perceptive of the reactions of others, and considerate of the needs of others are the ones who seek to share gratification rather than having as their goal their own gratification only.

No adjustment is going to be possible unless dissatisfaction is brought into the open. If you have differences, you must discuss the subject with your husband even though the idea of talking about it may seem disagreeable to you or to him. There is no need for this to be a distasteful topic. It is an accepted fact of life, just as birth or death, and therefore cannot be hidden by not talking about it.

A satisfying sex relation is one of the positive elements contributing to the well-being of each partner and of the married couple. The partners who find satisfaction together in the sexual relationship are more likely to have well-integrated personalities and a home in which their children will find happiness. Just as we appreciate good food and comfortable shelter, a workable philosophy of life, and the security of religion, so we recognize that sex fulfillment in marriage is a positive good.

Part Three

THE MOTHER

CHAPTER TEN

Is It Parenthood vs. Romance?

I HAVE often been asked if pregnancy makes any difference to a marriage.

It certainly does. It changes many aspects of the marriage, and in the beginning the conception of a child calls for some real readjustment in thinking by both husband and wife.

Today the average husband is as interested as his wife in finding out all he can do about what is going on during pregnancy. Here is a list of things that a husband ought to be told when his wife is pregnant for the first time:

1. He should do all he can to share her experiences by becoming informed; read the books on this subject that she reads, go to parents' classes with her, and talk to her doctor about the impending birth.

2. He should do his best to understand her.

3. He should help her follow her doctor's advice, particularly his advice on diet.

4. He should try to shield her from anxiety and fear and try to reassure her when she is worried. He must expect

some temporary change in her emotional reactions. Changes in sexual desire, for instance, are not unusual during pregnancy.

5. If hospital and doctor permit, he should try to stay with her at least part of the time during her labor. This is when she is going to need him most.

Those are some of the things he can do. There are also some things that he shouldn't do. For instance, he shouldn't think of his wife as being in a "delicate condition." If he starts acting as though she is going to break in two at any moment, she'll soon begin to think the same way. At the same time, he should not expect her to be exactly the same as before pregnancy began. He must remember that she is going to tire more easily, and during the early months, while she is adjusting to pregnancy, her moods are going to swing far more greatly than usual. Extreme emotional reactions are not at all unusual in pregnancy. And while these may be hard on him, they are easier to bear if he expects them and tries to understand them.

He should not be too anxious about her condition and should not exhibit undue alarm if she manifests some adverse symptom. Being anxious is not going to help her at all; instead, he should talk to her doctor. Another thing that he should not do is ask family or friends for advice. If their advice were good, they would be practicing obstetrics.

As far as you, the pregnant one, are concerned, remember that it is not rare for pregnancy to be accompanied by tensions and generalized anxiety. We are taught in our culture to look upon pregnancy as a happy occasion, as the beginning of a new and better life. We venerate motherhood. But in spite of all this, and our desire to believe in it without reservations, pregnancy does bring with it some uncertainties and doubts.

Although we try to leave them unmentioned, they do exist. Medicine has eliminated most of the risks in childbirth, but there is still an underlying fear a woman feels when the time of delivery comes.

Part of this uncertainty is worry about the baby. The first thing a mother does when she sees her newborn child is to check fingers and toes and body and sometimes ask the doctor for reassurance.

Motherhood implies a different life pattern. It means awakening at two or three in the morning to quiet a cranky child, changing diapers, and being totally responsible for a helpless human being, not only through its infancy, but for the rest of your life. There is nobody who can really take over the role of mother for you, with all the care that it entails. It means these kinds of changes as well as being able to watch a cooing, happy baby. So, along with all the happiness that motherhood can bring, there are also difficulties that must be faced.

To be less than ecstatic over the prospect of pregnancy is behavior that is not approved by society. But the feelings of the uncertainties are still there. And because the expression is repressed, the mother-to-be can easily start to develop feelings of guilt. She can develop feelings that she is not a proper mother. This is arrant nonsense, of course. Is it really wrong to feel annoyed that your growing stomach limits the dancing you enjoy so much?

Much of the resentment is momentary, but trying to

171

stamp it out makes it linger much longer and it permeates your whole outlook.

Pregnancy and the ensuing motherhood are not total joys. Let's be very honest and frank about that. And the more you can take a practical and realistic attitude toward these two phases of life, the more balanced you will be.

One of the real difficulties in pregnancy is correlating the attitudes of husbands and wives. It takes a bit of doing on everybody's part. About those strange cravings — for lobster and ice cream, or maple syrup and dill pickles, for example:

Perhaps many years ago women were more apt to have physical needs which caused them to have strange cravings during pregnancy, but now, when a woman is under a physician's care and watches her diet and has additional vitamins, the cravings are psychological and a bid for attention. When a wife does have these well-known cravings, it would be a good idea for her husband to humor them, knowing that he is doing just that. Humoring these requests for strange foods makes a wife feel specially pampered at a time when she is a little fearful and can use some extra attention and comfort.

This is one chapter of the book that might be read aloud to your husband — at least in part — for you should not forget that a man's reaction to pregnancy is quite different from the reaction of any woman.

I'll never forget one incident that showed a man's reaction. It happened in a large department store rather early in the morning when the crowd was small. I was standing near an escalator and noticed a woman moving down the stairs. She was quite obviously pregnant and within about

172

a month of delivery. As I looked away I saw a floorwalker looking up at her, terrified, his mouth halfway open, spell-bound. As she came closer he became more agitated. When she stepped off the escalator he almost lunged to her side, ready to catch her if she fell. She walked away quickly, but the floorwalker stood for a while to recover his composure. It had been terrible for him. The poor man obviously thought that the woman was going to slip, fall, and have her baby right there in his department. This would have been a crashing experience for him: an infant born in gen-tlemen's accessories.

This story points out one attitude that almost every man has toward a pregnant woman. He simply does not know what to expect. Taxi drivers, bus drivers, even waiters and clerks, make no secret of their desire to avoid the pregnant woman and the consequences she might bring.

Most men feel that a woman who is wearing maternity clothes might have her baby at any moment.

Also, men look at a pregnant woman in a different way. In a slim skirt and sweater, I am sure you became used to long, admiring, imaginative observation. Now you receive furtive glances. The man looks long enough to identify your maternity clothes, then looks quickly away.

He might also look at you rather knowingly and grin. But this look is also a popular, nearly universal, natural experi-ence, and no man's look of accusation should trouble you for long.

If the man is more a friend of the family than a casual observer, he will keep his eyes averted and be overly con-cerned about you. Perched uncomfortably on the edge of a chair, he will be ready to leap to his feet and run to fetch anything from a glass of water to edelweiss. Women have told me they sometimes had the feeling that they were viewed as avenging goddesses who might throw bolts of lightning if their every wish was not instantly granted. This role pleases some women, but others become very self-conscious or even giggly.

Naturally, the more pregnancy a man has seen, the less sensitive he is about it. But the less experienced show symptoms of fright, panic, and discomfort, or completely detach themselves from the situation. These last try to appear so far above your obvious condition that you will become even more aware of it.

As to your husband's changes in attitude, be prepared for them with *his* first baby.

Traditionally, a man discovered that he was going to be a father when he came home and found his wife knitting booties, but modern women are more diverse in the way they choose to break the news. I heard of one man who came home and found his wife standing in front of a full-length mirror in a bathing suit. When he had finally assured her that she did not look different, she told him why she had reason to. So the glad tidings were out.

Life goes on about the same for a while. Then you will notice that your husband keeps watching you as though he expects something unusual to happen. Anyone who is watched constantly and secretly may become suddenly amused. By controlling yourself you may be able to keep from laughing out loud, but you will smile rather vaguely to yourself.

That does it. The vague smile has an entirely different meaning to your husband. Right then he knows that something is going on inside you, something magical and metaphysical that he will never understand. You are thinking something, you know something. From here on he is completely baffled and out of his depth. He becomes restless. He knows by your appearance that you are very busy, and he feels there is something that he should be doing.

A nesting urge sweeps over him. This takes many forms. One man I know decided to soundproof every ceiling in the house. Another had the urge to dig, and plowed up the entire back yard before he strained his back. Still another decided to paint. He had one room nearly completed when his wife noticed the odor and ran screaming out of the house. She called him from a neighbor's to explain that the paint odor made her feel nauseated.

Along with this nesting urge comes the protective urge. When you are out walking, he glares back at people who stare at you. By his manner he is defiantly saying: "This is all perfectly natural and none of your business."

Of course if no one is paying any attention to you and he does not have to be defensive, he becomes isolated. He will saunter along with a casual air and act as though you are really his sister-in-law whom he hardly knows at all.

I have seen men become entirely left-footed when their wives were pregnant. In their awkward desire to help they made vague boosting gestures, wanting to help their wives upstairs but not knowing where to take hold. At a party the same type of man will hover around with his hands in his pockets or hanging in mid-air. He will occasionally pat his wife's shoulder and smile at her or will gently pull her skirt down over her knees. The whole effect is one of complete helplessness on his part.

It is a rather ungainly time for both of you just before the first baby comes. But because of the experience a bond may grow between you. And about the time you are ready to accept the whole idea of never returning to normalcy, nature steps in and rushes you off to the hospital. Within a few hours you face an entirely new set of problems.

I believe the fundamental reason for these attitudes on the part of the man is this: He cannot give birth to a child and you can. There is always a mystery about any special ability.

When that fateful moment does come and you know that the baby is due, how well prepared are you? Largely, of course, this is a matter between you and your obstetrician. But I have often been asked to discuss the question of natural childbirth.

Actually, many obstetricians and gynecologists have quite openly pointed out that natural childbirth suits only a relatively small number of women. It takes a special temperament and a special outlook. Many women have a low pain threshold and suffer severe pain during prolonged labor of more than twelve hours. Such suffering is needless. It can possibly even be harmful. And frankly, there is no way to predict your own limits of endurance.

In recent years a strong objection has grown to the publicity that has been given natural childbirth as being a great experience. So many women have felt that they would have missed something unless they had their babies by this method. As a matter of fact, a recent prediction in the medical profession was that the boon in natural childbirth is going to collapse very soon. Doctors who have seen how patients talked themselves into childbearing without anesthesia are now beginning to talk them out of this. They feel that there may be psychological damage when a woman who has trained for natural childbirth finds, at the end, that she needs an anesthetic. She may feel that she has been defeated. She may feel that she has disappointed her husband and her doctor. And she may also feel that she has missed the true joy of childbirth. A large percentage of those who try natural childbirth do fail to go through with it.

Should any complications arise during birth, only a patient who is anesthetized is immediately ready for whatever medical measures may be deemed necessary. On the other hand, with the patient who is going through childbirth naturally, the doctor can lose precious time, and this is important to the health and safety of both mother and child.

Most obstetricians agree that the physical and psychological preparation for labor and delivery which is stressed in the natural childbirth program is an asset to any expectant mother. The labor of an informed and relaxed patient is apt to be easier and shorter than that of a tense and terrified one. But, medical men have pointed out, there is no reason for women to feel that they must turn their back on medical aid and advances when it comes to birth itself. One reason for the popularity of natural childbirth was perhaps the desire on the part of some women to belong to the "group" — that is, the tendency to want to identify with other people. Such a group, or club, had members who had an unusual experience in common and they could talk about it. Once it was fashionable for a new mother to say she didn't feel a thing, but now it's become the vogue to have felt everything.

Some doctors feel that the natural childbirth method is primitive. They have compared the withholding of anesthetics during delivery to waiting for the crisis in a pneumonia patient instead of administering a shot of penicillin. And doctors feel that it isn't necessary for a woman to go through such an ordeal in order to appreciate what she gets afterward.

So perhaps the interest in natural childbirth is fading away.

But whatever course you decide to follow, let me emphasize one point: Go to a doctor in whom you have complete faith.

Patient confidence is vital in any medical situation. In fact, when an ailment is *psychosomatic,* confidence in the person who is treating you is more important than any medicine that can be prescribed.

Having a baby is certainly not an imagined complaint or illness. It is all very real. But the relationship between the doctor and the mother-to-be is sensitively personal. Every woman comes to depend on the doctor who is going to deliver her child, possibly more than she depends upon her husband at this time. So I repeat, you must find a doctor who gives you a feeling of *complete* confidence.

Each general practitioner or obstetrician has his own methods. The doctor prescribes what he believes is right for each special case. Each mother is different and each baby is different, so the treatment has to be different.

Of course the experience is not unique at all; in this country a child is born at least every half minute. Some mothers are placed under sedative the moment their pains begin and wake up with a child in the nursery. Others feel every moment of labor and even watch the process of delivery in a mirror above them.

In childbirth, some doctors believe that suffering is "natural," and I have heard the term "beautiful" as a part of what a doctor calls "the *miracle* of childbirth." Some women do get a deep satisfaction from pain. After it they feel purified. It is just as true that some people, men and women, seek out situations that are guaranteed to make them suffer physical or psychological torture. We find this drive for self-punishment in people who try to demand radical surgery and in people who have automobile accidents so they can endure an agonizing recovery. Their motives are unconscious, but the need for pain is there.

I am sure it is no surprise to you that doctors are human, too, and thus subject to the same mental quirks that affect the rest of us. Dr. Karl Menninger, in his book *Man against Himself*, points out that he has been impressed by the failure of some surgeons to understand or sympathize with the suffering or fear of their patients. But most physicians today are anxious to use pain-relieving techniques unless there is a good *medical* reason for not doing so. For example, patients with heart or lung conditions cannot tolerate certain drugs. In the case of childbirth, a doctor may feel that an anesthetic would endanger the life of the child.

179

If you cannot come to an understanding with your doctor, investigate others through the county medical association or, if you wish, write the American Medical Association (535 North Dearborn Street, Chicago 10, Illinois) and ask for a list of specialists in your area.

As a final word, let me make this point: There is a very different kind of apprehension of childbirth experienced by first-time mothers and mothers who have had children. The mother-to-be does not know her ability to tolerate pain or how painful the experience will be to her.

However, if a woman has known labor and delivery, if she has tried a certain philosophy and method of childbirth, then she has some basis for judgment. The medical help she selects and the procedure she and her doctor agree to follow are *her decisions*. She must be satisfied with that decision because she must answer to herself when the time of delivery comes.

So it is your responsibility to commit yourself to what will happen. You have many choices and should make yours an *informed* choice. When you arrive at the hospital, your baby's arrival is only a few minutes or hours away; *then* is no time to *change your mind*.

Having had your baby, then what, as far as your husband and your romance with him are concerned?

In the majority of cases childbirth interferes with normal sexual relations only for the period demanded by the physician in the interest of your health as a woman. But in some cases childbirth leads to what has been called postpartum maladjustment. After the birth of a child a woman may lose her interest in physical love for a short time.

180

There are any number of reasons why a woman loses interest in sex for a time — or sometimes, unfortunately, even permanently — after the birth of her first child.

A very young girl who has the responsibility of wifehood as well as motherhood may not be prepared emotionally for so much. She may feel that she is tied down irrevocably and will never have the chance to have the fun out of life that she thinks she would have had had she not married so early. And so in some way she feels as though she can punish both herself and her husband by not enjoying sex any longer. It is true that she emotionally punishes herself and hurts her marriage, but this is a situation that is not irrevocable and it is one that can be overcome once she realizes the potential danger to her marriage of such behavior.

The second common cause of this sudden aversion to sex is that suddenly, having found herself a mother, she may fear becoming pregnant again. Perhaps her pregnancy and delivery were not quite as comfortable and easy as they should have been.

Whether it is a fear of having more children or whether it is the resentment of having had life suddenly burdened with responsibilities, a woman should try to readjust her thinking in relationship to the sexual happiness she and her husband had before the baby was born and try to achieve that sexual happiness once again.

If this loss of desire should happen remember that, after all, you do love your husband. This is the man you loved before you married him — loved enough to marry him. This is the man you loved early in your marriage, and this is the man you still love. The sexual act is a part of love. No mat-

181

ter how you look at it — from the man's point of view or from the woman's point of view — they are irrevocably tied to each other. A man looks at the sexual act as an expression of his love. A woman looks at the sexual act as a part of her love.

Nonetheless, both of you realize that this is an outward manifestation of the deep emotional attachment you have for each other. The coming of a child should not hinder this attachment and sever it in any way. It should actually strengthen the attachment you have for each other both emotionally and physically.

If you suffer postpartum maladjustment, I suggest that you discuss this problem with your doctor just to make sure that there is no organic problem that may be causing you unwarranted pain in your sexual life now that the baby has been born. This is always a slim possibility.

Discuss the problem quite fully with your doctor. Let him understand how you feel about your husband — after you have managed to understand yourself how you feel about him.

The physical expression of love is a very important and a very beautiful part of married life. Don't let an unwarranted emotional feeling — a feeling of being tied down to responsibility too soon or of fearing the added responsibility of more children — stop you from continuing in the beautiful relationship you have had with your husband.

CHAPTER ELEVEN

Children and Happy Home Life

CHILDREN DISRUPT the carefree romantic relationship that existed between you and your husband. Even though children are the blessing that cements the ties of marriage, they make necessary a readjustment in your marital behavior. There is seldom time for spontaneous impulses of love during the daylight hours and no lovely, lazy embraces on awakening, even on weekends. At night there is the nagging little fear of the child awakening to call for its mother.

Until the arrival of children, both husband and wife have each other's undivided attention when they are together. After your husband's exclusive possession of your affection, it is only natural that he should feel a twinge of resentment or even jealousy — when you devote yourself to the children's needs. This is one of the initial resentments that some fathers have when a new baby comes into the house. As a matter of fact, mothers are encouraged to get their husbands to participate in the care of the baby. We are told that Daddy should change the diaper once in a while, give the baby a bath, feed him, make his formula. But all the adjusting seems to be called for on the part of the father.

Too often the art of pleasing a man goes out the window when the stork flies in. In today's homes (which are so much smaller than they used to be when we were children) there is a great deal of emphasis on large areas where the family gets together rather than emphasis on privacy and your own room, as it was at one time. In many homes today a closed door is unknown. The danger in the current campaign for more wholesome and shared family life is that it ultimately results in making parents feel guilty if they try to have a private hour by themselves.

But that is not all. The end of romance in marriage is often the result of many subtle changes in the woman herself. She allows these changes to come over her along with the new cares of motherhood. How often have you permitted yourself to be found in a house coat and slippers at the end of the day? And does your preoccupation with what your child is being so quiet about in the next room show on your face when your husband is talking to you about what happened to him at the office? Have you ever met your husband at the door after the children have been indoors all day in bad weather with a wild look in your eye and a dramatic cry of "You take over, I've had it"? And is dinner-table conversation limited to the behavior reports of the children and perhaps the gossip of the neighborhood?

A woman may feel that a man can expect nothing more. She may feel that she waits on him and has the children to look after and just hasn't time to put on a dress and that there is nothing else to talk about but the gossip since she has been cooped up in the house all day. What happens is that all this combines mysteriously to have a dampening effect on her husband, or at least on the would-be lover that lurks within him. He becomes bored. Boredom means the very death of romantic love.

What can you do about overcoming these difficulties that children can cause?

Don't let your job of homemaking run over into your husband's free time at home. He looks forward to coming home to a wife, not to a distracted housekeeper.

Indulge your strictly female interests in your children's antics and recipes and gossip, but do it with the other women during the day. Try putting on a dress and freshen your make-up, and perhaps even put on a touch of perfume in time for your husband's return from the office.

The second thing you can do is to make sure that your children learn quickly that you and your husband aren't always at their beck and call. They have to understand that you have rights that have to be respected too. They should regard your room as private property — not to be entered without express permission.

Plan ahead to ensure time of uninterrupted privacy with your husband. When you are out in mixed company and other wives are revealing their marital age by entertaining with humorous anecdotes at the expense of their husbands, why don't you speak up with a quiet plug about one of your husband's assets? Watch his eyes meet yours with a rush of affection.

It all adds up to offering your husband only your best self. Forgo the luxury of indulging in moods of irritability, discontent, and envy. These are luxuries. It means one more strike against you in your effort to keep the one irreplace-able treasure — your husband's romantic love.

Of course any woman who is cooped up indefinitely with young children can expect to have the shakes, if not a few bruises. You may experience battle fatigue if you are on the firing line from six-thirty in the morning until seven at night. You may get nervous jitters from too many bowls of cereal dumped on the kitchen floor, the constant roar of the wash-ing machine, the patter of little feet running away from a broken lamp in the living room, and the deafening thump on little toy drums that good old Uncle Charley sent the children for Christmas.

When this happens, it may be a wonder that you are still on your feet. But if this is your problem, you may take comfort in the knowledge that you are not alone. Millions of other women are being exhausted every day by a brace of inexhaustible, pre-nursery-school youngsters who never run down — but their mothers do.

Children encourage what some experts have called "woman's greatest enemy" — that is, "female fatigue." Most women are completely uninformed about this condition, although it may occur a number of times during a normal life.

Female fatigue may be expected whenever a woman ex-periences a great biological change, such as when she reaches adolescence, is pregnant, and when she is in her menopause. Each of these periods demands violent en-docrinal adjustment in the body. While this redesigning takes place, she is not up to her usual pace.

For example, a building that is being reconstructed inside

may look the same on the outside, but the demands upon it will have to change while all the activity is going on in the halls. The work will start gradually, as does female fatigue. It will reach a point where the work inside may slow to nearly a halt. Then as the work is nearly completed, the effects will gradually go away.

This is an absolute fact of nature. But most women bravely hang out a "business as usual" sign and try to keep up the pace they established when no reconstruction was going on.

It is also an absolute fact that this enforced slowdown comes at a time when there is a desired speed-up.

A girl from twelve to seventeen is anxious to sprint through all kinds of school activities and social fun. And, to her, the idea of going to bed early three or four nights a week is square with sharp corners. It's a ghastly drag.

A woman who is pregnant with her first or her sixth child has more to do than she ever dreamed. It is usually called "getting ready for the baby," and she bustles like a lady robin carrying sticks and straw in a high wind. Unlike the robin, whose babies are on their own when they can fly, the mother with several youngsters has a variety of external demands to speed up, while her internal demand is to slow down. This pushing and pulling would strip a machine's gears, and something similar happens to a mother. She comes to the delivery room a nervous wreck, believing that several days in the hospital will give her a needed rest and make her ready to go back to building pyramids. But she is not ready and will not be until the biological changes are completed. The "expectant" mother expects too much of herself. She must rest during pregnancy and afterward. She must slow down, even though everything around her says speed up.

Between forty-five and forty-eight, women experience the biological changes of menopause, right at the time the children are on their own and she has the opportunity to speed up her social and community activity. Everything around her says, "A new world is opening to me," and her mental attitude says, "This is the end of the world." Again rest becomes important. The push and pull that threaten to strip gears must be overcome by meeting the pressure in a relaxed state.

Adolescents, pregnant women, and women experiencing menopause are victims of female fatigue that has a biological basis. There are psychological causes too. Job insecurity, an unfaithful husband, the rebellion of children, the dawning realization that the dream life may not be realized — all these can make a woman despondent and nervous.

As I have said, rest is a potent cure. Also, good professional counsel can often find the cause and get the problem down to normal size.

The problem for the young family with a new child — or even with more than one child — is to adjust living conditions so that neither family life nor the romance of marriage suffers. Here too often it is the romance that gives way, when it should be just the other way round.

Take a very simple set of circumstances. For example, you, as a mother of a ten-month-old child, are still rocking the baby to sleep. It annoys you, it annoys your husband,

and it takes a great deal of your time and energy too. But what do you do about it?

This habit of the child is well established. In fact, the habit is even older, because the baby learned to like to be rocked even before he was born. The motion of your body as you walked was comforting long before you even met him. Since birth you have continued to comfort him in this way. If you look at it from his point of view, he has every reason to demand to be rocked.

Do you have to stop this habit?

The answer is no, it is not absolutely necessary. You can walk and rock as long as you are physically able to carry him. But this is an effort for you. At the end of the day, when you are tired, you are wearing yourself out completely and you are probably wearing a groove in the bedroom carpet. So there is no real reason to *stop* the habit, but there is no reason why you should *not* as long as the baby's need for loving and physical contact are satisfied some other way. Cuddle your child and give him your loving warmth before bedtime, and this will probably satisfy him.

Breaking this habit of needing to be rocked is one of many adjustments you and the child will have to make. The time will come when the child is better off to be trained to a cup and must be weaned from the bottle or breast. At another time toilet training is required. Someday your son will be forced to speak words to get what he wants instead of making gestures and meaningless sounds. These steps are all part of a child's development and growth.

There *are dangers* involved when you stop rocking your child. He will sense that he is being denied an expression of love and comfort that he had learned to accept as due. This is why some compensation, some substitute for this lack of loving, is required.

You might try rocking at any other time except bedtime. Then he will associate rocking with playtime rather than sleep time.

When you make up your mind to stop the rocking habit, be sure you do not *change* your mind. It is very cruel to be inconsistent. If you happily rock your son one night and absolutely refuse the next, what is he supposed to expect? He will get the idea that he can cry and you will finally give in. If you do comply some of the time but not all of the time, he will be very angry when you refuse. Once you have decided not to rock him for bed, never do it again.

This means tears.

I recall one doctor's advice that may be helpful. The baby who needed rocking was a third child. With two other youngsters and a home to care for, the physical strain of rocking was almost too much for the mother. She talked to her doctor and he gave her this prescription: "Put the baby down, close the door, and take care of your other children for a while. Whatever you do, do *not* go back in the room while the baby is still crying. Endure this medicine three times a day for ten days and then call me."

The medicine worked in *eight* days. The baby was going to bed calmly without rocking *and without tears.*

Part of what happened with this prescription happened to the mother. When she did not have to face the chore of rocking her child she became more relaxed, and as a result the baby enjoyed her more. When the rocking was a necessity the mother resented it and began to show her anger toward her child in many ways. When the habit was broken both the mother and child developed a much better physical and mental attitude.

It is difficult to endure the screams of a frustrated child. But it is even more tragic to see a one-year-old disliked by her parents because she is harassing them with demands to be rocked or walked.

A great deal of a mother's responsibility is to the child, but do not neglect yourself or your husband. The hostility that can be developed in a family if an infant is insisting upon special treatment can be much worse than the unnerving sounds of a sobbing child.

As children grow they do not stop needing attention. Quite the contrary, the amount of attention children will demand from their mother depends almost entirely on how much she is willing to give. And here you run a danger of overextending yourself in their behalf and forgetting the partner in your marriage. Your problem is to be sure you *remain* a woman, just as alluring, feminine and interesting to your husband as before the advent of the child. That, in addition to your responsibilities as a mother, will give you a very, very full-time job.

Now let us suppose, that you have survived the four years after your one-year-old was broken of the rocking-to-sleep habit. But now you have a five-year-old who wants you to play with him, to do everything with and for his amusement.

191

It is typical for a five-year-old to demand attention; it is not atypical for the five-year-old's mother to require attention too. By now the bud, if not the bloom, is off your marriage. If you were a working girl before your wedding you had a feeling of stature and independence. Now this is completely gone.

By the time a child is five years old you have gone through almost the same routine every day for five years, so it is not surprising that it fails to stimulate you. You undoubtedly feel you are more capable than this work demands. You can make more important decisions than what to have for dinner or whether to use the blue or the green tablecloth. If you did not spend some time with the adult friends during the day you are sick of small talk from a small child. And as you look around you, you cannot see much change ahead except that you will be a day older at sundown. With this attitude it is easy to see why a five-year-old's play does not interest you. It is possibly a bitter reminder of your oversimplified, statureless life.

I can give you some reassurance. This situation will change. Around six your child will step into a world with much wider horizons. He will realize that parents are only two of the "big people." There will be teachers, librarians, policemen on the corners, the school-bus driver, and he will be trying out his personality on all of them. His life will be involved with many new friends and probably a handful of enemies. So home will not be as important. Mommy and Daddy will not be as important either. With this whole new world around him it will be less important for him to be Mommy's playmate, admirer, confidant, and friend. In fact,

Mommy will be in for some direct and critical comparison with the teacher, the librarian, and many other female "big people" whom he meets. Your son will learn that there are other ways of doing things, not just your way. He will learn that he can make other friends and find other people to play his games. This growing away from dependence on Mother is normal and healthy for the child.

It is remarkable how many mistakes mother love will atone for, and it is also remarkable how many different ways there are to handle the problems that arise between parents and children — all of them quite proper solutions, depending on the families and the personalities involved.

CHAPTER TWELVE

You and Your Child's Personality

MOST MOTHERS are ambitious for their children; they want Junior or Judy to be physically well, attractive, and bright. They feel superior when the youngster shows himself to be precocious in walking, talking, and growth, and inferior and unhappy if he seems outstripped by a neighbor's child or some other youngster of his age.

The important thing for young mothers to realize is that children develop at different rates of speed. Though Johnny next door may be saying "Mama" or "Daddy" while your Billy still is experimenting with nonsense syllables, your son may later start speaking in complete sentences and leave Johnny behind!

While there is no set timetable for a child's development, general guides can give a mother at least an approximate idea of the progress of growth over a period of years. Such books as Dr. Gesell's *Child and Infant in the Culture of Today* and *The Child from Five to Ten* can be most help-

194

ful to the intelligent mother. They give her a basis of meas-
uring her child's growth — not against that of a certain other
child, but against the general growth pattern of most children.

Most children are not ready for *formal* learning until they
are six years old; our public school system recognizes this
by not attempting formal learning before first grade. This
does not mean that the four or four-and-a-half-year-old is
not *capable* of learning. He is learning all the time.

You'll probably notice that your child often asks "Why?"
or "How?" about apparently trivial things that come up
during the day, and he listens to the answers. It's important
that his questions be answered fully, for this curiosity is a
desire to know and learn. He probably likes to be read to
and often may ask for the same story again and again. By
repetition he becomes familiar with words, and later he'll
be able to incorporate them into his growing vocabulary.

One four-year-old boy I know, fascinated by cars, has
learned to recognize and name at least a dozen different
kinds. You see, the child at this early age does learn things,
but generally they are things that interest him or things he
can use.

Look for opportunities in the natural events of the day
that will give your child a chance to learn informally. For
example, if you put on his shirt, count each button as you
button it. If you're going to fix bacon for lunch, ask him
how many pieces he would like and let him take them from
the package, counting as he does.

Children learn better when learning is associated with
pleasure rather than with pain or pressure. To spank a child,

for example, because he seems not to be interested in learning teaches him the negative fact that learning is connected with punishment. This could very well carry over into his attitudes during his school years and cause him considerable difficulty.

I have often wondered whether parents today really understand what is meant by spoiling a child. We hear so much about giving our children love and affection and freedom to express themselves and the importance of sparing them insecurity and frustration that the question often arises quite legitimately, "Can all this be done without spoiling the child?"

It seems somewhat contradictory, on the face of it, to give a child so much and yet not spoil him. It also seems to be true that many parents these days will frequently express some alarm over the fact that their children are so assertive and demanding. Parents feel that they, as children, were not nearly so outspoken and precocious, nor did they have so much.

There is no doubt that the position of greater importance that we accord to our children these days does in fact have a great deal to do with this attitude. However, the child who makes his presence felt is not necessarily a spoiled child.

The first thing we have to do in connection with the problem of the "spoiled child" is to define our terms. We often call a child spoiled if he is petulant and whining and constantly demands attention. Also, if his gratitude is short-lived and suggests the fact that he accepts as ordinary what we like to consider indulgent or special, then we think that the child is a little spoiled. However, closer examination of these shortcomings obviously points up something in addition.

The spoiled child hangs onto his parents and is childish in his inability to take no for an answer. As a result, he whines and cries for things as though life itself depended on getting them. This is quite different from being assertive. An assertive child may also sulk in response to denial, but he is independent enough to find other things that please him. The spoiled child does not enjoy this flexibility and freedom. If anything, he tends to put all his eggs in one basket — that is, childishness. He is, therefore, rigid and uncompromising as an expression of his own emotional immaturity. Being spoiled is only a part of the more general pattern of his adjustment.

You prevent your children from being spoiled, or correct them if they are, by encouraging their emotional growth and independence. It's almost impossible to spoil a child during the first year of his life. However, you can effectively sow the seeds for this unhappy eventuality.

The mother who is overprotective and who watches her child twenty-four hours a day, constantly fussing and amusing him, can exaggerate a child's normal dependency. It doesn't take more than two or three years for a child to recognize that his mother feels threatened if he should carry on or display his temper. Under these circumstances, not only is the child tyrannized by the impulsive character of his desires, but so is the mother.

Assertiveness, too, should be brought under control so it

197

does not make slaves of either you or your husband. But first let's understand from the child's point of view what makes a child overly assertive.

Let's see if we can imagine a situation that would make a "no girl" out of you. Let's say that you have always been very good and obedient and passive. You are small and rather timid. Suddenly you get fed up and decide to see if you can behave the way you want. You have always been afraid to say anything but yes. Then one day you said no and got away with it.

This gave you a great feeling of power, so you began to assert yourself more often. The experience was exhilarating. You were not punished as you always thought you would be, and you were actually having a wonderful time doing what you wanted to do.

Every youngster goes through a time in his life when he becomes almost completely assertive. The child tests the boundaries on everything until he knows exactly how far he can go. This is quite natural.

It is also natural for teen-agers to check their boundaries and for wives to check their boundaries. If any individual is oppressed or restrained long enough, he will finally lash out just to see how free he can be. Literature is filled with stories of the hen-pecked husbands who defy their wives, dominated wives who defy their husbands, and downtrodden nations that revolt against their oppressors. These are all stories of people or peoples who are making a bid for freedom.

I am sure you see how you could become a "no girl" if you were placed in the circumstance of finally trying to gain freedom you had never known. It is quite possible that you too would overdo the noes, just to prove you could get away with it.

You could also become a worm who is turning if you were oppressed. Many mothers do not realize how often they say no to their children.

Activity, exploration, testing the limitations — all are vital to a small child. A little girl wants to try to do everything her mother does. Mother dusts, uses the vacuum sweeper, washes clothes, mixes a cake, and her little girl begs to try each job. To you, as the mother, this seems impractical, if not impossible. In dusting, the child could break a lamp or an ash tray. In using the vacuum, the youngster could scratch and even break the furniture. In washing, there is no question that soap would go on the floor. In cooking, dough would be splashed all over the kitchen and wasted. So in the interest of practicality, efficiency, and speed, you say no.

These are only a few examples. There is sewing and bed-making and drawer-straightening. With Daddy there is painting and raking and lawn mowing and ladder-climbing and even digging in the dirt.

Think what a "no girl" you would be if even in your own home you were not allowed to participate in the activities. I believe it would become perfectly natural for you to say no any time anyone wanted you to say yes. The frustration would be so great, the denial so constant, that you would make "no" your habit word too.

What can you do to get a child out of the "no" rut? The answer is to handle each problem affirmatively. Let your youngster know quickly and consistently what the limitations are. Establish rules for her behavior. Instead of making it necessary for her to ask and you to say no many times on one subject, simply make a rule and say "Never."

Do this only if you mean never, and do not create rules for some days that do not apply to other days. A child needs to hear yes many times more than no. When you make your rules, be sure that the youngster realizes that there are many more yeses, many more things she is allowed to do, than there are things she must never do.

As to the daily noes that are said around the house, try to avoid the need for them. If you are going to make a cake, you must realize that your daughter will want to do the same. So get her an apron, a deep mixing bowl, and a child-sized spoon. Give her some dough of her own and let her go to work on it. The chances are she will work a few minutes and become disenchanted. Then she will be off to play with the dolls or her cat. Once she is satisfied that she can do it if she wants to, her desire will not be so great. The result will be that one yes will eliminate ten noes and perhaps a tantrum.

When Dad hauls out the ladder the youngster will want to climb it, so Dad should be ready to guide Junior up and down one time just to get it out of both of their systems. Most children thrive in a yes atmosphere. And this is no more than an attitude of understanding. The fact is, Baby must touch, no matter how often Mother says no. The fact is, a child must paint or hammer or climb a ladder whether he knows how or not. This is a fact because children are "doers." They are always active mentally and physically.

They always want to participate in what is going on at home.

And remember that all children between two and a half and three years go through a phase of saying no to everything. They grow out of it if you don't push them too hard.

Another problem that may disturb you greatly is the vile temper your child may exhibit from time to time.

Many children have "tantrums," which are their way of relieving tensions. Yes, children have tensions too. And they have to find a release for these tensions, just as we must find releases for ours. Many times the child's method of releasing these tensions is unpleasant or disturbing to others (again, like many adults). In young children, these outlets sometimes take the form of temper outbursts, fingernail-biting, thumb-sucking, and throwing objects.

Often these releases occur more or less regularly. Some parents feel that their children act this way because the child is frustrated. Others think their child is insecure, unhappy, or even maladjusted.

Many mothers and fathers blame themselves. They feel that they have failed somewhere, because they are sure the well-adjusted, secure, happy child just wouldn't behave this way.

I can't agree. Of course some mothers and fathers increase the tensions of their children by failing to provide a warm, happy, secure environment. But even the child who is getting along well will have the need for a tension outlet. Even a happy child can have tensions.

Adults are lucky. When we feel tense we can have a cigarette or go for a walk or do one of a hundred things to calm down and relax. When a child releases even normal tensions he or she does so often by indulging in so-called "bad behavior."

Nine out of ten children outgrow these habits and find other emotional releases which do not annoy or disturb parents as much. However, children have a knack for finding outlets that bother parents.

There are very many behaviors children use to release tensions, from temper tantrums to being destructive, to running away from home, to stuttering.

And how does a mother cope with them?

First of all, the best way to handle a temper tantrum is be sure you remain calm. If you can stay unemotional and go on doing what you have been doing calmly, as if nothing is happening, you will find that the tantrum is over much sooner and is less likely to recur as often. Many children give up tantrums if they find the tantrums do not get them anything. It will take several trials before the child learns this, so don't be too impatient.

Even more important than what you do when your child behaves in this manner is to attempt to discover what caused it. It might be useful to keep a record of your child's activities so you will more easily be able to distinguish the behavior pattern (most children follow a pattern).

Frustration is one frequent cause. Quite often a child becomes more easily frustrated when he is tired. During a period of fatigue your child may react violently to situations that would not cause such a reaction during a time when he is well rested.

Whatever the cause of a temper tantrum, the best way to put an end to it is ignore it, difficult as this may be.

What you may want to do, of course, is spank the child to relieve your own emotions. It will do that, certainly, but as a method of getting children to behave, spanking has definitely been oversold. It doesn't end a temper tantrum or make a child quiet and good or kind and unselfish. It doesn't always make him obedient, either. It may suppress the bad behavior, but that is all. And most parents, when they stop to think, realize that spanking has no special magic, after all. It just doesn't accomplish the purpose.

There are no doubt some happy homes and some well-behaved children where spanking is used. There are also families — and I believe they are more successful in the long run — where, in spite of a flock of high-spirited youngsters, spanking just isn't done.

Actually, success with children doesn't depend on whether you spank or whether you don't. In fact, it doesn't depend even on the right methods of punishment. It depends primarily on reducing occasions for punishment to a very minimum. That means that you must understand your child's needs. Children who are truly enjoyed by their parents are seldom chronically naughty. On the other hand, children who are just one more thing to worry about are going to be naughty a great deal of the time.

If a child seems to need spanking or other punishment too often, it's a good idea to ask yourself what causes his irritability and his bad behavior. The child who fusses at mealtime and refuses his food may be better off if you just take the meal away and say nothing. Doctors today advise offering, not forcing, food on a child and caution against insisting that children eat everything. Children who are restless and wriggly in public places perhaps shouldn't have been taken shopping or visiting in the first place. If you have to take them along, try to schedule some activities they think are fun. Don't just do the dull things that have to be done. You can always stop for a moment at the pet-store window where the kittens and puppies are playing. Or stop and look at the building excavations where the steam shovels are digging up the earth for a foundation. Give the children a few moments to enjoy these. It may take more time on your shopping trip, but it's worth it.

It's perfectly true that children do need control. A child whose parents constantly let him run wild or disobey is going to be an unhappy child. And inwardly he is going to blame his parents for his unhappiness. But there aren't many cases of disobedience that can be cured by spanking which couldn't have been handled by a firm and friendly "No" or "You must."

The first thing you should do is to understand your child's childishness. Make time for fun for him. Then be firm and remember to act promptly. Keep up your good humor as well as you can, and I assure you that you are going to get things done quietly and without fuss, without anger — or spankings.

Times have changed and so have the methods of child care. We now are aware of many of the details of the child's emotional life that our parents and grandparents didn't know. We no longer agree with their emphasis on physical punishment. We feel the discipline they gave was successful, but at the child's expense. He began to fear punishment. His wilder impulses were restricted, true, but along with them parents also restricted his imagination and curiosity and his intellectual expressiveness as well as his capacity for enjoyment.

Even though we no longer depend on physical punishment, this doesn't mean that we should go to the other extreme and let the child go without discipline. A child needs to feel that his parents, however agreeable they are, have their own rights and know how to be firm. He must know that they won't let him be unreasonable or rude. He likes them better that way, and it trains him from the beginning to get along with other people.

One question that comes up time and again among parents involves the special problems of the destructive child.

Many children go through an aggressive and destructive stage. Some children going through this period have carried their destructive feelings as far as hitting unsuspecting guests from behind.

I read recently of a case where a three-year-old managed to knock out his aunt with a well-placed vase to the back of her head. I don't know if the child was attempting to eradicate his aunt or merely break the vase, but he nearly succeeded in doing both. Even if your child limits his destructive energies to inanimate objects, it is little consolation to you and your husband.

Some children seem to be destructive accidentally — that is, they seem to be "destructive prone" — they seem to get into trouble without really meaning it. No matter what they do, they break things or mess things up. If this is the case, there are some very simple precautions you might take to attempt to reduce the casualty list of your household goods.

First of all, check through your home for things that are in reach of your child and that may be broken or be used by the child to mark or break larger and sturdier objects. These things should be moved and put out of reach so the child won't get mixed up with them.

Next, secure all doors with locks that are out of reach or too complicated for your child to open or close. If you have a large fenced-in back yard let him spend a lot of time in it, running, climbing, and playing with messy things, such as mud. It is also a good idea to let him hammer with a rubber hammer in the yard as much as he wants, but these activities should always be done when you or some other adult is nearby to supervise. Inside the house, attempt to prevent accidents before they happen by discouraging activities that lead to trouble. Don't let your child bounce balls or hammer in the living room, where such activities may produce a broken window or a three-legged chair.

Anticipate what may happen in advance. Don't trust to luck or a last-minute scream of "Don't" to prevent your child from releasing the stuffing from the sofa with a pair of scissors he never should have been allowed to get hold of in the first place. You must realize that children are naturally careless and curious, and the value of material things means little to them. Fortunately for all of us, most children learn to outgrow this attitude.

Whenever possible, have different adults take care of

your child. Your disposition will be improved (only a mother can fully realize how tiring the constant supervision of small children can be). Try to convince your husband to help take the load of supervision off your shoulders whenever posible. You should also avoid taking a destructive child into public places or a friend's home where his behavior will be likely to cause a good deal of trouble and embarrassment for you.

Some children seem to destroy things intentionally. While the things I have already mentioned apply to this type of child, there are some further things you might try. Dr. Nina Ridenour, in an excellent pamphlet available from the New York State Society for Mental Health titled *When Your Child Is Destructive,* suggests the following for handling an intentionally destructive child:

If your son crumples up his father's newspaper or is careless with books, try substituting a paper or book of his own which he may crumple to his heart's content. If he is in the habit of tearing his books, give him books made of durable cloth until he is old enough to handle the other kind in a gentler manner. To keep him out of your bureau drawers, the safest thing to do is to lock them if you have the kind that lock. If not, put things that are important to you in the upper drawers that he can't reach. You should also provide him with a chest of drawers or cupboard of his own where he can keep his own things. If he insists on drawing on the walls even after you've provided him with substitutes, the best thing to do is to provide him with a wall of his own in his room on which he may scribble. This

207

wall should be covered with beaverboard or paper or some other material that will prevent the wall from being permanently damaged.

If he pounds on the furniture, try giving him other things to pound on. Hammer and boards are excellent if you have a place that is out of the main living area, such as a back yard or recreation room, where he can work. If not, modeling clay is very poundable. If he likes scissors and uses them destructively, get him a pair of blunt scissors (sharp scissors should never be given to children under any condition) and provide him with his own paper and cloth which he can cut. To keep him out of your pocketbook, give him one of his own to carry around. You will want to fill it with things so he won't feel that it is a fake, and you will probably find that your child will prefer a discarded pocketbook of yours to a new one of his own.

If your child loves messes, give him messy things like clay and sand and finger paints to play with. Needless to say, this should be done with adult supervision. And last, one of the best remedies for children who destroy things is to give them materials and objects that you are willing to have them take apart.

Most children who destroy things always have a reason for their behavior. It may be caused by jealousy of a sister or brother. It may be because the child is frustrated by your restrictions or by his own failings or inabilities. Try to find out why your child is behaving as he is and then try to remedy the situation.

In your discipline, be firm, consistent, and explain the

reasons for your rule. Give your child permissible outlets for his behavior until he has matured to the point where he becomes constructive instead of destructive.

Both you and your husband will have to expect a good deal of wear and tear on all parts of the house until this maturity develops. Try to meet it with patience and understanding. You must remind yourselves that in a child's growth the negative usually precedes the positive, and destruction comes before construction. Some of the most destructive children later grow up to be the most creatively constructive adults, if you can hang on long enough to see them grow up.

Another matter for despair in parents involves the manners of their child.

What our parents called manners is nothing more than common courtesy. In short, it's consideration for others. No matter what a child does in life or to what the child aspires, he needs manners. Unless they are taught to some degree to a child, he is impossible to have around. No matter what you hear to the contrary in some of our child-centered homes, a polite child is a delight.

The polite child usually is also happy and is not at all frustrated. Surprisingly, he often thinks adults are nice. He thanks people because he feels grateful. He is considerate because the grownups in his world are considerate of him.

A child should start learning manners as soon as he can see and hear. He should learn them at home. What he sees and hears there, he will emulate. If he has to wait to learn politeness elsewhere, his politeness will always seem mechanical and varnished and forced, as though he were polite for an ulterior purpose (which is generally true under these circumstances).

By the time a child is two or three he should be able to say "thank you" and "please" almost routinely. And he will say them routinely if you say them routinely to him. When he forgets to say them, all he needs is a reminder. By the time a child is four he should greet all adults politely as a matter of fact — either with "hello" or "good morning" — or a similar greeting — with a handshake. He should be taught that adults do not bite and will usually give him back a smile as warm as the one he gives them. By the age of four he should know enough to hightail it for home the minute his friends are called indoors for lunch or dinner or when his friend's father comes home. This is the first rule, by the way, on how to make your neighbors love your children. By the time a child is six his table manners should be sufficiently tolerable that he chews with his mouth closed at least part of the time. And he should know when and how to use a napkin, know that a knife is for cutting food rather than the table, and that his feet are supposed to be under his chair and not reaching eagerly into space to kick shins.

By the time a child is ten, at the latest, he should learn not to interrupt, no matter what a strain it is on his patience. If he must break in, he should preface it with an "excuse me." He should wait until all are served at dinner before eating. (And it would be heavenly if he would, at the age of ten, remember just once to hold the door open for adults to enter first or to close it after himself.)

210

These are a few of the social graces whose use endears children to tired grownups and the absence of which makes children intolerable. Any parent who wants a polite child can have one. It just takes time, patience, and a million reminders. The million and first time you may reap the reward.

Then it's worth the effort.

Other specific problems I want to deal with here are lying, thumb-sucking, and the sexual adjustment of the child, for all of these have come to my attention time and again as matters that disturb mothers.

Let's take them one at a time.

When a child tells an untruth it is worrisome, and it may be infuriating. But before you lose your temper, remember one thing:

Children aren't born truthful; they learn gradually.

Children learn less from punishments and sermonizing than by living happily among people who value honesty and practice it themselves. The small child often tells tall tales because at first he scarcely knows the difference between fact and fancy. This is hardly lying; yet parents can help him take another step in his inner growth by getting such a child gradually to see that this difference does, in fact, exist.

"That's *quite* a story," you might say. "Now see if you can tell me what *really* happened."

The older child knows much more clearly what's true and what isn't true. But under some circumstances the older child gets carried away by wishful thinking until he almost believes his own stories. For example, a youngster who is

211

really afraid to stand up to his more aggressive friends may amaze you with tales of his own heroism. He just beat up the neighborhood bully, he announces, and then he offers all the gory details. You may fall for it once, but then you begin to catch on.

Though this is usual enough, a mother might do well to ask herself why it is that this particular child needs to boast. Is he jealous of a brother or sister? Is it hard for him to make friends? Is he physically awkward or slow at the skills in games that most youngsters set store by? Does he, perhaps, generally feel inferior?

If so, help from parents at crucial points is what is called for even if it takes some extra time and planning. You will need to be patient, too. It's not easy to enjoy the company of your most difficult child as much as that of his easygoing brother or his charming little sister. Can it be that there is some foundation to his feelings that you like him less than the others? Making friends, learning to be brave — these come more easily to some children than to others. Quieter games or play with one friend at a time may be a better answer for the timid youngster than trying to get him to be one of a gang of small ruffians.

Older children often lie because they feel the weight of too heavy demands. They dread parental criticism, sarcasm, or indifference if they fail. When a boy is held rigidly to high marks at school or a girl meets with no sympathy in her adolescent agonies and ecstasies, neither one is likely to be honest in his or her dealings with Father and Mother. Instead, they will probably retire into a world of their own where parents are seen as enemies rather than friends.

212

When children are untruthful, punishment alone is rarely the answer. Punishment only adds to the feeling of loneliness and the conviction that nobody understands. The only way to make lasting changes is through improving relationships. To accomplish this, parents must try to meet the young person sympathetically on his own grounds. This doesn't mean letting him do everything just exactly as he wants. It does mean encouraging him to air his gripes; it means a listening ear when he does it. It means a genuine eagerness to meet a youngster halfway, to work out differences in the open wherever possible and, when you decide that you must hold your ground, explaining your reasons for it.

You must have gathered by now that it's quite normal for children to lie, especially if they live among people who lie as a matter of course. The youngster who realizes, for example, that in her household accountings Mother is less than frank with Father, or that her dealings with neighbors are marked with petty deceits, is hardly likely to value honesty. The son who hears his father boasting of pulling a fast one on a business competitor will soon learn the art of double-dealing too. When you are trying to teach respect for truth, even the white lies that fall easily from your lips set your children back.

It's also normal for everyone to lie once in a while when the temptation to get out of a tight spot is especially great. Though you certainly shouldn't sanction this by finding it clever or amusing, neither need you be too self-righteous. Who of us hasn't succumbed to this sort of thing?

However, what is not normal is that kind of constant,

often senseless lying that grows worse instead of better and threatens to become a part of the whole fabric of a child's personality. For this kind of lying there is no single explanation or cure. The causes lie very deep. These are the hard-to-reach children; they are baffling to both their parents and to their teachers. Yet below the surface they are often deeply troubled and unhappy and wishing they could change. Yet they feel helpless. These children are psychologically sick and are fortunately the exception. For them you do need the help of a psychiatrist or psychologist — often for a long period of treatment. When the home climate is healthy, however, most children learn to tell the truth — slowly, perhaps, but surely. Some learn faster than others. But eventually, in a family where feelings and affections are warm, where truth and fair dealings are honored, they do learn. Eventually, the standards of parents become truly a part of themselves, and "conscience" is born.

Thumb-sucking can be as annoying as fibbing, as any mother knows.

But sucking is a very natural reaction in a baby. For the first months of his life the sucking action is the only way that the child gets food. But it's more than just a way of taking nourishment and it continues throughout life to be pleasureable in itself, especially during the first year. Observations of infants and young animals seem to show that they don't thrive well if they aren't allowed to follow their natural impulse to suck. Babies get restless and irritable, and some scientists have observed that young animals which are fed entirely from medicine droppers tend to be sickly and behave abnormally. So within the first year or so a child should not be discouraged from thumb-sucking.

As a matter of fact, in the early months the child may not get enough sucking even though he is being bottle-fed or breast-fed. Sometimes a child feeds very quickly and needs extra time for sucking until he is about a year old. If your infant is still on the bottle, you can prolong the sucking time by using nipples with smaller holes or by giving more feedings or by using a pacifier. You can't be certain, however, that this extra sucking time will cut down the urge to suck the thumb, but it's worth trying. Attempts to break your infant of thumb-sucking could make him irritable and angry at this point, and all it will do is increase the nervous tension that will help him prolong the habit of sucking the thumb.

Let the thumb-sucking alone, but encourage him to be active and to explore his world. Give him plenty of space to crawl about in. Give him safe things to handle, and by all means let him put them in his mouth if he wants to. Give him hard food and objects he may bite. Talk to him as much as you can and play with him. As the baby uses his mouth more and more for biting and his hands increasingly for play, he is likely gradually to give up sucking his thumb.

By the age of three thumb-sucking is usually tapering off. But a great many three-year-olds still suck their thumbs at times, particularly when under stress or when angry or worried or when going to sleep. There are still a number of children who suck their thumbs at the age of four. But nothing should be done about this unless the child spends

215

a large part of his time with his thumb in his mouth and isn't active and interested in play with other children his age. In that case, I would examine his daily life to see if he is physically sick or bored or unhappy. Or perhaps he isn't getting enough chance to use his mouth in eating or biting and sucking. He may also need more personal attention from you — more encouragement toward active satisfying play. If he defeats your best efforts and continues to draw into himself it might be helpful to get professional advice.

Thumb-sucking in an older child may mean that the child is still holding onto a habit he really doesn't need or want. If this is the case, he may stop if you occasionally remind him in a friendly way. As he gets out among other children and begins to feel the social pressure against a babyish habit, he will be as eager to give it up as you are to have him give it up. Perhaps he'll suck his thumb only in secret then. Sometimes an older child sucks his thumb for the same reason that the three-year-old does. More than ever, you are going to need to try to find what's keeping this child from enjoying play with other children.

Thumb-sucking has nothing to do with enlarged tonsils or adenoids. There are many disagreements on the effects of thumb-sucking on the shape of the mouth and the teeth. During the period before the second teeth are forming, thumb-sucking doesn't seem to do much permanent damage. Even if the baby teeth have been somewhat distorted, the jaw tends to right itself later on as thumb-sucking tapers off. Scientists who have studied the subject most carefully usually agree that strict measures to stop thumb-sucking only increase a child's tensions and make him crave his thumb more than ever.

Now, as to the very sensitive area of children and sex, here a mother can have an important and almost frightening influence on the future attitude of her child toward the entire reproductive process.

As a general rule, you should tell children what they need to know, when they need to know it. For example, when a neighbor or a relative is going to have a child and is obviously pregnant, one of the youngsters is going to ask: "How come?" To sit a five-year-old down and explain every step of intercourse, conception, and gestation would be ridiculous — just as it is ridiculous for a five-year-old to be told he was brought by a stork, in a doctor's black bag, or appeared in a rose or a cabbage. It is probably enough to say that the baby is growing inside the mother, and that the mother will go to the hospital and have the baby and bring it home.

Children are quite aware of growth. This idea is well expressed in a book called *Sex Attitudes in the Home*, copyrighted by the National Board of the Young Men's Christian Association. The author explains that youngsters are well adjusted to the idea of themselves as being littler. They see pictures of themselves as infants and realize that they will someday be as big as Daddy. It is easy to explain to a child that he was once so tiny he could grow inside his mother. He knows chicks break out of eggs so does not have much difficulty accepting the possibility that a lamb is born from its mother alive, and so is a child.

If the youngster has an acceptance of his own body as

217

being beautiful rather than an object of shame, he or she will be able to accept physical experience and contact as adults in marriage.

Boys and girls realize early in life that they are different. This can be explained very casually. Boys have organs on the outside, and girls have organs on the inside. To young children this is perfectly acceptable and as far as the facts need to go.

Embarrassment of parents when they are telling their youngsters about their bodies and about sex is almost disastrous to the discussion.

You find out a great deal from your family. Even if the subject was taboo in your home, the very fact that it was, told you a great deal. If the subject could never be discussed, it told you your family was very self-conscious about the facts of life. As a result, you may have been a very inhibited bride. I receive many letters from young girls who were too curious because they were not told enough. They experimented — and now are sorry.

The truth is that the facts of life are observed by youngsters. They see pregnancy. They see tiny babies. They notice the difference between boys and girls. They talk among themselves. So no child can actually be shielded from the facts. What the parents can do is help their youngsters avoid too much curiosity, too much fear, and a wealth of misinformation.

What all parents try to do is this, and I want to be very candid: *We try to keep our children from having babies before they are married*. We try to preserve our children's health and our daughter's virginity. Now how can this possibly be done without a certain amount of discussion? How can a girl learn the case for chastity if no one explains the value of virtue to her? How can a boy or a girl know the dangers of venereal disease unless they are explained? How can we keep children from becoming so stimulated erotically that they cannot avoid intercourse, unless we tell them that this point of stimulation is a possibility. Almost the most important question, how can we expect them to believe us and respect us if we have not been honest and candid with them since they asked us the first question?

If you feel you need help in what to say specifically to a child, let me suggest *The First Facts of Life for Children*, published by the Child Study Association of America, and the "Sex Education Series" pamphlets of the American Medical Association. Also, your library will have many books on the subject that will be helpful.

And finally, in relationship with your children, enjoy them. Don't try to stop them or speed them up. Just keep them going ahead, straight and confident of the future. That way lies happiness.

Part Four

EVERYWOMAN

THERE ARE some problems, situations, and influences that are common to almost all women today, so let's generalize and for a while consider Everywoman.

First of all, there's the question of beauty. I have mentioned it before, but I'd like to return to it here, for beauty can be, and often is, the most important attribute of a woman. Usually when I talk about beauty I am not thinking in terms of physical beauty alone. I am referring to the over-all beauty of a woman, including the beauty of her inner self, and I have discussed this in connection with the single woman. But for a moment I want to examine the dangers and challenges of physical beauty as such.

From across the room (and that is how we all meet each other — from a distance), a beautiful woman is the essence of womanhood. To a man she embodies everything he desires. To a woman she is someone to emulate, a symbol of what she herself should be, of what is the ideal for all women.

Yet the next step in meeting someone is to *talk*, and what the beauty says may not be beautiful in the least. She may be an animated magazine cover but as shallow as the page she would be printed on. If you are that girl — and there are hundreds of you — who is interested only in herself and behaves coldly or in a superior fashion to other people, you have failed to meet the challenge. If you are ruthless about

223

what you want and committed to sleazy values, you have failed even more sadly.

I believe that any beautiful woman or handsome man has the responsibility of living up to the perfection of body that he or she was *born* with. Others have to work hard to be attractive or even acceptable. So having been endowed with beauty at birth, the possesser has a lot of spare time to develop what goes on inside, to perfect inner potentials. Many beautiful people, however, are idolized as children and learn to expect favors. Even if they are not self-centered, less attractive people will assume they are spoiled and pampered, and although they resent it they tend to join the pampering. I've heard beautiful women who also have real substance object to that fact. People spoil them whether they want it or not and make them feel completely unequal. People may often hate them, too, for something they cannot and never could control: their attractiveness.

Commercialism is another factor that threatens the beautiful woman. Beauty is a very salable product. And where there is marketable merchandise, there will be salesmen. These peddlers convince a girl that she should have a career, that she will rise like a rocket. They capitalize on her and build her *need* for approval. At the same time, and for an obvious reason, there are people who are anxious to pay to see a beautiful girl, whether she is a singer, dancer, actress, or a model in a photograph. The reason is almost always sexual attraction. Beyond this, however, is the age-old idea that the beautiful are good and the ugly are bad. So there may also be the attraction of goodness. On an even deeper and destructive level, there is the neurotic need of

224

some to see the *good be bad;* that is, to see unattainable beauty appear to be available and subject to humiliation. This is the mechanism at work, for instance, in strip-tease audiences.

So for beautiful women there are constant temptations and dangers — and the final, almost certain consequences of old age. When a life is built exclusively on face and figure, the possessor is driven to preserve these foundations. But face and figure *will* show the signs of age, and each wrinkle will be a new frustration.

The truth is that no woman, whether she is a beauty or just an average girl, can ever be secure unless she develops an inner quality, an assurance that is independent of her outer appearance. This is the beauty that is important in the second stage of any meeting. Beauty and homeliness show across the room. The inner quality shows in communication, in actions, in living. This quality may be difficult to develop, but this will be what you *have* after beauty has faded. And when a woman has this quality, physical beauty becomes secondary and strangely unimportant.

Besides beauty, there are a number of other concerns, conflicts, and circumstances that women share, perhaps without realizing how common they are to all women.

Take moods and weather, for example. Did you know that your behavior, your disposition, your health, even your efficiency at home or on the job, are often tied to the day's temperature, barometric pressure, humidity, wind, and sunshine?

Lately climatologists have made a number of new findings about you and the weather. When the barometer drops and the day is cloudy and very humid, you may find your-self in a foul mood. What's more, your husband and your children may also be unusually "difficult." The fact is that the pressure in the atmosphere affects the pressure in our tissues, and the result may be a throbbing toe, an aching head, or an unlocalized case of "nerves." The physiological effects of weather, and especially of sudden changes in it, have actually been observed by scientists: our pulse rate, blood pressure, body temperature, metabolic processes are all subject to the whims of weather.

So if at times you feel unusually tired or grouchy or "put upon," just stop and look out the window for a moment — and instead of blaming your husband or children or friends, admit that you're simply "under the weather." And then take comfort from one certain thing about it: it will change.

Insomnia is another common source of very real dis-comfort, but not nearly so mysterious or uncontrollable as the weather. Unfortunately, however, it seems to become aggravated rather than relieved by familiarity. If insomnia becomes a habit, we become frantic, try one remedy after another, and often make sleep less probable than before. Still, insomnia is also something we can cope with — and conquer — if we really try to understand it.

Some people would like to lie in bed forever. They be-come so exhausted at the thought of sticking their toes out from under the covers and getting up to face the day that they roll over and go back to sleep. Yet the same people, only a few hours before, found their beds hostile, uncom-fortable places where they could not rest. What these slug-abeds are saying, morning and night, is: "Oh how I hate to face what the day may bring. Oh how I hate to face reality."

Many women, without knowing it, resent the fact that they have to work. They want their husbands to take care of them as their fathers did when they were little girls. Getting out of bed means that they must leave the protected world and get out into the cold of the working world. The bed creates a feeling of being a coddled infant again. This is why eating a sandwich and drinking a glass of warm milk before retiring helps some people to go to sleep. It re-creates the feeling they found most comforting as infants, when they could not rest easily until their tummies were filled.

So if it is necessary for you to earn your living and provide your own protection, it would be well for you to think about your circumstances honestly and positively. I have talked to many women who said they hated their work. When they were questioned in detail, it developed that there were many points about their jobs that they liked. The fact that they had to work at all is what displeased them. If you suffer from insomnia, are you perhaps being childish and unreasonable about the realities of life?

The middle of the night is a lonely, depressing time. Often twenty-five minutes of sleeplessness will seem like hours. Some people seem to choose this time to think about the mistakes they have made during the day. They worry about finances, about the past or the future, and their bodies tighten up with anxiety. Most of what goes on in their minds either cannot be anticipated or cannot be helped. So they waste what little energy they have left and make it impossible to relax enough to renew their energy. And then the fear of sleeplessness is added to help keep them awake. They start worrying about not sleeping, exclaiming, sometimes aloud, "I can't go on like this much longer. I've got to get some sleep."

This pattern can become very difficult to break. You may have to begin by learning the physical art of relaxation. When you get into bed, close your eyes and make yourself as comfortable as possible. Then concentrate on relaxing your body. First make sure the muscles of your jaw are not clenched. Let them sag. Move your head about until your neck is completely relaxed. Next, see that the muscles in your forehead are smoothed. Your eyelids should feel so heavy that you can't open them. In this way, take an inventory of your entire body. Relax it one section at a time, all the way to your ankles and toes. This exercise may not put you to sleep the first time, but each time you do it you will feel yourself becoming drowsier and drowsier.

As you relax this way, you will be concentrating on your eyelids or ankles, not on your unpaid bills or on what may happen tomorrow. If troubles still crowd into your mind, visualize yourself in peaceful surroundings. Remember a day at the beach when you were lying on the sand. Daydream yourself into a pleasant setting, and real dreams may follow.

When you wake up in the morning, do something pleasant as a treat. Spread some special jam on your toast or take the time to read a chapter in a new book. Be sure to plan this reward and make some preparation for it just before you go to bed. With this pleasure in mind you will have something to get up for.

The idea of bribing yourself to get out of bed or of doing exercises while flat on your back before you go to sleep may seem quite foolish to you. But if you have tried all sorts of other remedies and nothing has worked, you might as well give these methods a try.

Some women lie awake at night — and also go around being depressed all day — because of a feeling of inadequacy in handling people. Instead of letting yourself be saddled with such a burden, here is something to remember about people: There are many today who are disturbed, who have difficult personalities. No matter what you do or who you are, you are bound to come into contact with examples of these. The unfortunate thing is that they make your life less pleasant.

The first thing to learn about difficult people is that there are various types of them. Some are more difficult than others. A few may be genuinely sick, while others are in only a temporary lapse from their more normal and agreeable selves. Generally there are three main types of difficult persons. The first type can be called schizoid. These are the unadjusted people of the world who are not at ease with the environment that has been forced upon them during their lifetime. They are not deficient mentally. They may even be especially bright. And they seem to be able to obtain almost anything they want — with the one exception of adjustment to the world.

The second type is called cycloid. They are excessively moody people. You can't depend upon their moods, however. On one occasion they are gentle and gracious and buoyant. You like them a great deal. But the next time —

229

maybe even a few hours later — they are just the opposite. They're cranky and sullen, silent and bitter.

The third type is called a perverse personality. These are the ordinary difficult people. They are the ones you probably deal with most often, and frankly, they are the most difficult to deal with because they are, as labeled, perverse. They will argue and refuse to co-operate with you. They are just plain contrary — or ornery.

There are many degrees and forms of perverseness. One of the most common manifestations is prejudice. People who are prejudiced cripple their personalities by being bigoted about many things. They don't like the members of another race or of a different religion, or they don't like men who are fat or women who are thin. The list is endless. If you have to deal with people who have prejudices, then you know how difficult they can be.

Still another difficult personality is the one that we call the egomaniac. This is the self-centered person who thinks that the whole world revolves around him and excludes everybody else. Then there are defeatists — the people who believe that the world is in league against them. Related to them are the negatives, who are opposed to everything and will always argue against the positive side.

Whatever the type, you can recognize a difficult person by the childishness of his behavior: he throws a tantrum, loses his temper, acts emotionally in a situation that requires reason and calm judgment. Because the tribe is so numerous, one of the first rules for living a successful life is to know how to handle these people. It isn't really hard if you master a few rules.

230

The first rule is to check up on your own personality to see that *you* are not being difficult. You yourself may unwittingly be expressing some perverse or schizoid traits! Be tougher with yourself than you would be with anyone else.

Another rule is not to let difficult people get under your skin. Look upon them as you would look upon children. With children you have to be patient, forgiving, sympathetic, and understanding. This is the way to be with difficult people. You will be surprised how well it works — much better than flying off the handle yourself.

Third, build up the ego of the difficult person, because that's where this person is mostly in need of help. This is, I think, the most important rule of all. It is the key for handling practically any difficult personality who edges his way into your life. When you analyze the cause of perverseness in the vast majority of the people who are difficult, you will find that it always seems to stem from a feeling of inferiority, and this inferiority may be years and years old. The person craves importance; he is suffering from what you might call ego-hunger. So feed his hunger, his ego. Then, for you, he will cease to be difficult.

An almost universally recognized and traditional, if not always truthful, feminine complaint is the headache. Certainly undue tension caused by worry will sooner or later give just about everyone a headache, but women seem to be even more subject to throbbing temples than men. Do they worry more? Perhaps — because they are not as likely to be able to *do* something about their worries, especially if they involve money and men themselves! Actually, though it may come as a blow to the male ego, women worry more

231

about money and about children than they do about men.

A study made some years ago showed that only about 3 per cent of all women reported complete freedom from headaches. And most of the victims of headaches said that they developed their headaches through worries — about half of them worrying about money and about an equal number worrying about children. Only 10 per cent blamed their headaches on their husbands, and here the problem seemed to be family argument rather than some other woman. Ten per cent blamed the noise of their own children and sometimes of neighbors. Other causes were health, jobs, and friends.

Oddly enough, the survey showed that suburban women are more frequent victims of headaches than are women in the city. Women who are under twenty-four seem to suffer more from headaches caused by worry and fatigue than older women do, and they develop them during the daytime and evening. Older women are more apt to wake up with headaches, although there doesn't seem to be any special reason for this. Maybe all of us who are afflicted with insomnia or headaches should try new pillows — a simple and obvious potential remedy, but then we so often overlook the simple and obvious answer.

On a deeper and broader level, all of us — all American women — have a serious dilemma to face at one time or another, and it involves our whole emotional lives.

On the surface, the American woman may appear debonair. Underneath, however, the typical woman is plagued by anxieties. Her desire for security and freedom and equality and happiness has led her into some frightening corridors. In many cases she feels a sense of fruitlessness and, looking ahead, can see only ominous possibilities for her future.

The main focal points for the dissatisfaction and frustration that seem to afflict so many of us today are the conditions and conflicts affecting sexual behavior and the conditions and conflicts affecting our place in the home.

Two wars within twenty years have caused a number of displacements and changes in social rules. Understandably, girls have been apprehensive about their marital futures as the marriageable men have been taken away from them. And the men, transported to alien lands and relieved of domestic responsibilities and community ties, have often become less stable in their relationships. In any case, it is a fact that there has been a sharp rise in premarital sex experiences among young girls and a corresponding rise in the rate of illegitimate births and abortions. At the same time, the divorce rate also continues to increase. Today one in three marriages ends in divorce, and the figures are rapidly approaching one in two.

Manners and customs change. It wasn't so long ago that chaperones were the order of the day — or especially of the evening. And an unfaithful woman was considered an outcast by the community. Now a girl is a bit ashamed to admit premarital virginity. She feels that it is a handicap and is in a hurry to cast it aside and be "grown up." Careful studies reveal that at least 25 per cent of married women commit adultery sometime during their lives. Wife swapping has become a game in certain suburban communities. We have pretty well beaten down the double standard. But evidently it hasn't brought us much satisfaction.

For at the root of casual and promiscuous sexual behavior there is obviously deep satisfaction and anxiety. A recent survey disclosed that more than 50 per cent of married women said they definitely were not well adjusted sexually in marriage. About 40 per cent expressed a deep longing for more affection, and 30 per cent confessed that they no longer found their husbands sexually attractive. What is wrong?

In our drive to break away from the supposed handicaps of being female, we may have lost sight of the risks involved. An illicit affair, an extramarital pregnancy leave deep and lasting emotional scars. And even if we haven't fallen into these traps, we may be carrying over our rivalistic attitudes, our struggle for dominance, into our sexual relations. Our accent on perpetual youth has also yielded some dangerous as well as foolish consequences. In short, we have won a number of battles, but we may have lost the war. Having rebelled against simple acceptance as a mate and ideal homemaker, we have cut ourselves off from a vital source of emotional support.

No simple solution for our sexual dilemmas can be offered. It certainly isn't enough to throw the problem to a young girl as a decision in personal philosophy. But what we can hope is that the present generation may have learned that the pendulum has swung too far in the direction of sexual freedom and license and should now start to swing backward. And through the understanding, companionship, and guidance of our own children we may be able to provide a more stable standard of morals for the next generation. Our influence through the formative years of development will remain the keystone.

As for the discontent and bewilderment that beset so many housewives who feel overwhelmed by demands and duties, it is surely no coincidence that their feeling of slavery has mounted with the increase in labor-saving devices. Grandmother may have had to heat water on a wood stove, but she didn't drive her children to school or shepherd them on frequent visits to a dentist. She may have made her own soap, but she didn't have to take the car to be serviced or summon a repairman to fix the washing machine and then spend time discussing the diagnosis with him.

The truth is that the devices themselves require attention, and with what minutes they do save us we rush to do something else. The absence of servants or of helpful living-in relatives is too obvious a change in conditions to warrant further comment. If you have complaints about your lot and yet feel guilty about them when you think of your grandmother, I have news for you. It won't ease your tasks, but it may ease your mind to know that *you* are undoubtedly doing more than she did!

Just recently a friend uttered this apt summary of her situation: "I expected to be a man-wife, but now I'm a house-wife." I imagine many women will echo this sentiment. But perhaps it's up to us to shift the emphasis, to reconsider the ways in which we expend our time and energy. After all, your husband may feel bereft and disappointed too!

Probably most troubling of all is the feeling many house-wives have that their efforts are not appreciated. Not only are the rewards few or seemingly nonexistent, but also the woman's position is given little or no respect. "Housewife" is not a glamorous occupation to record, and it becomes less proud when stripped of real authority and meaning.

Here again I can't offer a simple solution. How you cope with your problems depends on your own strength of will and purpose, your own integrity and courage. But under-standing the problems themselves, being aware of the chal-lenges and pitfalls, is a sound first step. And a knowledge of your own capacities, together with a conscientious effort to control your weaknesses and develop your abilities, will help you on your way. Just remember always that you are not alone. Other women share your troubles. And so do men. We're all human.

C2